the Way We Work

What You Know About Working Styles Can Increase Your Efficiency, Productivity, and Job Satisfaction.

Cynthia Ulrich Tobias

Best selling author of *The Way They Learn*
and You Can't Make Me

the Way We Work

**What You Know About Working Styles
Can Increase Your Efficiency, Productivity,
and Job Satisfaction.**

BROADMAN
&HOLMAN
PUBLISHERS

Nashville, Tennessee

Printed in the United States of America
0-8054-1833-4
Dewey Decimal Classification: 658.3
Subject Headings: EMPLOYEE—TRAINING OF PSYCHOLOGICAL
ASPECTS/LEARNING, PSYCHOLOGY OF
Library of Congress Card Caralog Number: 98-49513

Published by Broadman & Holman Publishers, Nashville, Tennessee
Editorial Team: Vicki Crumpton, Janis Whipple, Kim Overcash
Typesetting: PerfecType, Nashville, Tennessee
Illustrations by Big Cat Marketing Communications

The terms *Concrete Sequential, Abstract Sequential, Abstract Random,* and *Concrete Random* are
used with the permission of Anthony F. Gregorc, Ph.D.

First published by Focus on the Family, Colorado Springs, CO 80995.

**Published in association with the literary agency of Wolgemuth & Associates, Inc.,
Brentwood, Tennessee.**

Library of Congress Cataloging-in-Publication Data

Tobias, Cynthia Ulrich, 1953–
     The way we work: what you know about working styles can increase your efficiency,
productivity and job satisfaction / Cynthia Ulrich Tobias.
          p.   cm.
Originally published: Colorado Springs, Colo.: Focus on the Family Pub., © 1995.
     Includes bibliographical references.
     ISBN 0-8054-1833-4 (pbk.)
     1. Employees—Training of—Psychological aspects. 2. Learning, Psychology of. I. Title.
HF5549.5.T7T595   1999
658.3'124—dc21
                                                                                              98-49513
                                                                                                    CIP

1 2 3 4 5 03 02 01 00 99

DEDICATION

To my parents, Robert and Minnie Ulrich,
who have always believed the best of me;
my husband, John, who is my staunchest supporter;
and my twin sons, Michael and Robert,
who daily remind me that
there are truly no two alike!

TABLE OF CONTENTS

ACKNOWLEDGMENTS

I would like to gratefully acknowledge my family, friends, and colleagues, who keep me richly supplied with examples, anecdotes, and encouragement.

Chapter *One*
WHAT'S THE DIFFERENCE?

The account executive (AE) was about to close the deal. He could sense victory. But the client hesitated. "What are your rates?" he asked.

The AE smiled. This would be a piece of cake. "Well, it would, of course, depend on how long you want the ad to run and how big you want it to be."

"Just put me in the ballpark," the client said.

The AE's smile faltered. "Well, I really can't give you figures without more information."

"Oh, forget it," the client said as he walked away.

The AE felt frustrated. How could a client expect him to be specific about rates without giving him the facts he needed? But he realized that closing a sale was vital, so he sat down and developed a plan. When it was time to deal with the next client, he felt prepared.

"What are your rates?" the client asked.

The AE flashed a friendly smile. "Oh, I'd say an average ad campaign like yours should run between $1,200 and $1,400."

The client frowned and asked, "How do you know what I want? You haven't even asked me any specific questions."

Before the AE could recover, this client also walked away. The AE was frustrated again. Why hadn't he seen that coming? He sat down and reviewed the rates again, memorizing as many specifics as possible.

It didn't take long for his next client to ask the predictable question: "What are your rates?"

The AE smiled and then quickly and efficiently recited specific rates in each category.

The client looked exasperated. "Do you expect me to remember that?" he demanded. "I thought you'd have a rate card." And he impatiently walked away.

The AE sighed. How could he have overlooked the necessity of putting everything in writing? He carefully prepared a neat, concise, and up-to-date rate card. He highlighted the minimum amount of information needed, and then he confidently met with his next client. When he heard "What are your rates?" he immediately pulled out the rate card and reviewed the text.

The client looked disappointed. "But what would *you* do if you were me?" he asked.

The AE was taken aback. "Well, of course, I'm *not* you, so I couldn't presume to decide for you personally." The client was already walking away.

How could the same question carry so many different meanings? How could the AE lose so many sales even though he had tried to satisfy every need?

It doesn't take long, when you're working with any segment of the public or private sector, to realize that there are fundamental differences in the way people understand and communicate information. Each of us is "pre-wired" from the beginning with certain "bents" that influence how we decide what's important and how we understand the world. The best marketing packaging, the finest quality of product or service, can be perceived in entirely opposite ways depending on a person's point of view. These individual bents cause each person to be unique, and they often bring an overwhelming challenge to the arena of customer service and communication in the corporate world.

Often, with the best intentions, we chart a course and plan events in a way that makes sense to *us*. What seldom occurs to us is that other people may view the world quite differently. Therefore, it stands to reason that when we try to communicate with others, we're not all going to benefit from the same approach.

If you're like many busy people, you may become frustrated when you try to work with those who don't think the way you do. You may be convinced that they simply aren't trying hard enough. The fact is, however, that every person perceives the world through his or her own filter. Each is a unique individual with natural strengths and preferences. These individual gifts or bents are called *learning styles*.

Even when we accept the fact that each person is unique, it's often difficult to keep that in mind when we're trying to juggle the many demands of our personal lives and work schedules. Getting to know each of our family members, friends, and colleagues as individuals with unique bents is an exhausting but rewarding proposition. The busier and more complicated our lives become, the harder it is to remember that each person has a valuable contribution to make from his or her own perspective.

It's my intention to help you discover these different learning styles and to aid you in developing quick, practical ways of adapting your inborn strengths to the varied demands of learning and communicating—both on the job and in the rest of your life.

Few of us *intentionally* frustrate those with whom we work and live, but intentional or not, it happens. By reading *The Way We Work,* you can learn to identify many areas of frustration and conflict that can be directly attributed to a mismatch of learning styles. The challenge is to find positive ways of building on natural strengths without sacrificing desired bottom-line outcomes. Believe it or not, it *can* be done!

After reading this book, you will have gathered some very positive information to share with your organization. If you approach both management and staff with a positive attitude about learning styles, you'll be surprised at how open they are to discovering ways to value employees, vendors, customers, and others with whom they do business.

This book is just the tip of the iceberg about learning styles. In it I've highlighted the most practical aspects of five leading research models on the subject. You'll find the book to be an easy read, full of commonsense strategies and fresh ideas for immediate help in understanding and communicating with others. An annotated bibliography is included so that if you want more information, you can continue studying learning styles.

As you read, you'll see that several different learning style models are represented. If you've taken personality or learning style assessments before, you may have noticed you didn't fit neatly into any one category. Some people even test straight down the middle on every model, not showing any particular extremes in their learning style preferences. Everything you discover about your natural learning strengths should serve as a piece of the puzzle, not a categorical label for who or what you are. If, when you finish reading this book, you feel a bit confused about the labels, that's a positive sign that you won't just be "armed and dangerous," testing and labeling those around you.

Even though you'll find some potentially invaluable checklists and assessments throughout this book, you'll also discover that identifying and understanding individual learning styles is an ongoing journey of observations and impressions. As you read and begin to use these concepts, keep in mind the following general guidelines.

OBSERVE   Observe patterns of behavior. When you or your colleagues experience success, notice what the circumstances are that brought it about.

LISTEN   Listen to the way people communicate. If you only talk to others the way you want them to talk to *you,* you may discover you're speaking a language that's foreign to them. Listening carefully can teach you how you need to talk to them.

EXPERIMENT   Experiment with what works and what doesn't. Keep an open mind, and remember that even if an approach to learning doesn't make sense to you, it may work for someone else. We don't all learn the same way.

FOCUS

Focus on natural strengths, not weaknesses. Unfortunately, it's much easier to pinpoint areas of weakness that need improvement than to bolster sources of strength. But you can't build on weaknesses—strengths provide a much better foundation!

LEARN

Learn more about learning styles in general. Pay close attention to your own learning style in particular and how it affects those around you.

Everything you discover in this book is only part of the larger picture. There's much more to learn. While you're reading this book, look for additional pieces of your learning-styles puzzle. Resist the temptation to simply put labels on yourself or anyone else. No one should be boxed into any one learning style.

Once you begin discovering your natural strengths as well as those of your colleagues, you'll probably be relieved to learn that many of your differences have a lot more to do with inherent style than with any deliberate desire to annoy each other!

IN A NUTSHELL

Learning how to recognize and appreciate learning styles can help you identify the natural strengths and tendencies each individual possesses. As you read the following chapters, you'll discover positive things about yourself as well as your loved ones and fellow workers. This book is only the first step in your odyssey. As you keep observing and using learning-styles information, it will eventually become second nature to adapt and accommodate many different perspectives. Be patient with yourself, and don't worry about trying to formally identify people according to a particular learning style label.

Dr. Holland London, a seasoned clergyman and powerful communicator, spoke at a gathering I attended. In his inimitable way, he spoke on a variety of subjects in a short time with wit and wisdom. At one point he paused and leaned closer to the microphone. "People often ask me why I take so many detours when I speak," he said. "I just tell them it's because those I'm trying to reach don't live on the highway."

I sat there thinking about how hard we try to get people to move onto the highway so we don't have to put up with the inconvenience of detours. But perhaps instead of spending so much time and effort trying to convince others to move onto the path we've designed, we could encourage them to enjoy a few minor detours on the way to their destination. Who knows? We may even discover some places *we'd* like to travel off the beaten path.

Chapter Two

WHAT STYLE ARE YOU?

Послушайте меня

*A Russian phrase meaning
"Listen to me!"*

If I spoke to you in Russian but you didn't know the language, you wouldn't understand me. If I noticed your bewildered expression, I might slow down and repeat my Russian phrase more clearly and in a louder tone. But despite my best efforts—no matter how many times I repeated it, how well I articulated it, or how loudly I spoke—as long as I continued to speak Russian, the chances are pretty remote that you would understand.

How often have you heard yourself saying to someone, "How many times do I have to *tell* you this?" or "Didn't you hear what I *just said*?" The fact is, he probably did hear your words but didn't understand what you meant. Each of us takes in information in a different way, and because our learning styles are so diverse, sometimes we may as well be trying to communicate with each other in two languages.

Early in our relationship, my husband and I frequently struggled to get our points across to each other. One day he said in frustration, "I'm just talking to *you* the way I want you to talk to *me*." He paused and then added, "And I guess maybe you're doing the same thing."

For the first time, we both realized that the golden rule "Do unto others as you'd have them do unto you" doesn't always work when trying to communicate. If we only talk to people the way we prefer they talk back to us, and they're busy doing the same thing, chances are good that no one is truly listening. We haven't reached a common level of communication.

The Gregorc Model of Learning Styles

One of the most effective models for understanding learning style differences comes from the research of Dr. Anthony F. Gregorc. His model provides invaluable insights into how our minds perceive and understand information. Let's take a careful look at it.

PERCEPTION: *The way we take in information.*

We know people are not all alike. What we don't always realize is that each of us tends to view the world in a way that makes the most sense to us as individuals. This is called our *perception.* Perceptions shape what we think, how we make decisions, and how we define what's important to us. Our individual perceptions also determine our natural learning strengths, or *learning styles.*

TWO POINTS OF VIEW

Each mind possesses two perceptual qualities. They are *concrete* perception and *abstract* perception.

CONCRETE This quality lets us register information directly through our five senses: sight, smell, touch, taste, and hearing. When we're using our *concrete* abilities, we're dealing with what's here and now—the tangible, the obvious. We're not looking for hidden meanings or trying to see relationships between ideas or concepts. The key phrase simply stated is **"It is what it is."**

ABSTRACT This quality allows us to visualize, to conceive ideas, to understand or believe what we can't actually see. When we're using this abstract quality, we're using our intuition, our intellect, our imagination. We're looking beyond what is to the more subtle implications. The key phrase for the abstract is **"It's not always what it seems."**

Although everyone uses *both* concrete and abstract perceptual abilities every day, each person is more *comfortable* using one over the other. This becomes his or her dominant ability. For example, the person whose natural strength is *concrete* may prefer to listen in a direct, literal, no-nonsense manner. The person whose natural strength is *abstract* may often pick up the more subtle cues from others as they communicate.

My husband was driving on a busy Los Angeles freeway when I noticed a unique billboard and said to him, "John, look at that billboard!" John turned and looked. He looked and looked, and soon we were driving into someone else's lane of traffic. Horns were honking; people were shouting.

I turned to him and shouted, "John, watch where you're driving, for heaven's sake!"

He replied calmly, "Cindy, you told me to *look* at the billboard. Did you mean *glance?*"

I was exasperated. "Wouldn't you *assume* that?" I asked.

He shook his head. "I assume nothing," he said. "You said look, and I looked. The billboard hadn't done anything yet, and you didn't tell me what to look *for.*"

Although John's dominant style is more abstract, he was using concrete perceptions at that moment and had taken what I said at face value. It had never occurred to me that he would take it quite so literally rather than use his abstract perceptual ability to "read between the lines."

USING WHAT WE KNOW

ORDERING: *The way we use the information we perceive.*

Once we've taken the information in, we all use two methods of ordering what we know. According to Gregorc, the two ordering abilities are *sequential* and *random.*

SEQUENTIAL A sequential method of ordering allows our minds to organize information in a linear, step-by-step manner. When using sequential ability, we're following a logical train of thought, a conventional approach to dealing with information. Those who have strong sequential ordering abilities may prefer to have a plan and follow it rather than relying on impulse. Their key phrase is **"Follow the steps."**

RANDOM Random ordering lets our minds organize information by chunks and with no particular sequence. When we're using our *random* ability, we may often be able to skip steps in a procedure and still produce the desired result. We might even start in the middle or begin at the end and work backward. Those with a strong random way of ordering information may seem impulsive or more spontaneous. It appears as if they don't *have* a plan. Their key phrase is **"Just get it done!"**

At a recent workshop attended primarily by accountants and data processors, the participants were asked how many balanced their checkbooks monthly. The majority, of course, were careful to balance to the penny.

One man raised his hand and said, "I took the checkbook away from my wife." As the group frowned, he quickly explained. "We have checks that are a series of pictures. My wife was giving out her checks according to which *picture* she thought the person would like best. She thought that as long as all the numbers were

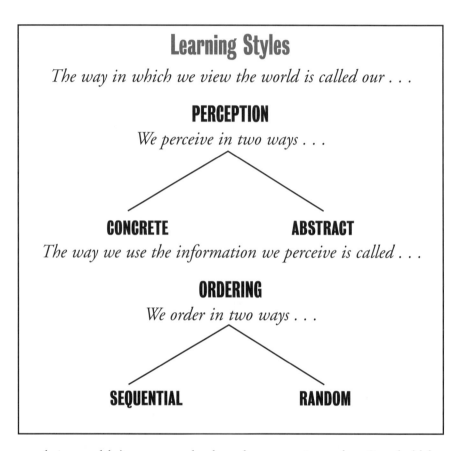

used, it wouldn't matter whether they were in order. So, she'd be at a fish market and say, 'Wait a minute, I think I have a picture of a fish on one of these!'"

The numbering sequence considered essential to this detail-oriented, sequential accountant hadn't even occurred to his random-oriented wife.

FOUR COMBINATIONS

When we take all of Gregorc's definitions and put them together, we get four combinations of the strongest perceptual and

Four Combinations

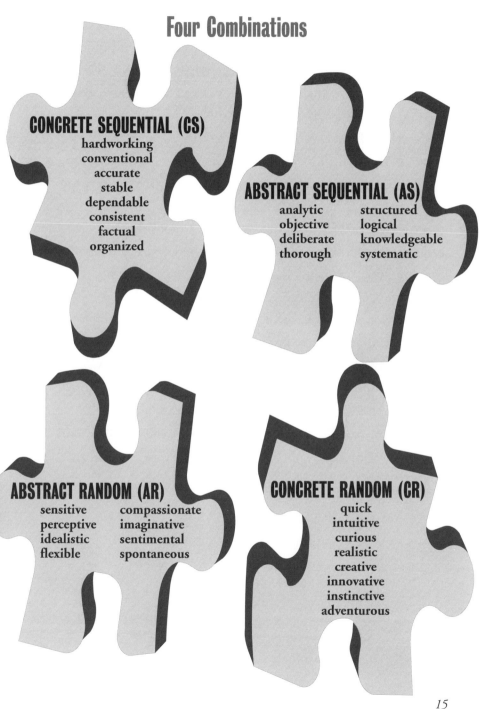

CONCRETE SEQUENTIAL (CS)
hardworking
conventional
accurate
stable
dependable
consistent
factual
organized

ABSTRACT SEQUENTIAL (AS)
analytic   structured
objective   logical
deliberate   knowledgeable
thorough   systematic

ABSTRACT RANDOM (AR)
sensitive   compassionate
perceptive   imaginative
idealistic   sentimental
flexible   spontaneous

CONCRETE RANDOM (CR)
quick
intuitive
curious
realistic
creative
innovative
instinctive
adventurous

ordering abilities. Remember, no individual is only *one* style. Each of us has a dominant style or styles that give us a unique blend of natural strengths and abilities. The chart on page 15 lists each of these four styles and their corresponding characteristics.

The following self-test gives some statements most often used to describe those who are dominant in each style. By learning some of the common characteristics of each combination (CS, AS, AR, CR), we can recognize and value what we like to do best and what comes naturally for us. We can also learn to identify and improve characteristics that we now avoid because we don't understand them well. Then, after we recognize our *own* natural learning styles, we can identify the differences with individuals that cause frustration and misunderstanding.

This test is a quick, informal method of identifying our learning style characteristics. If you would like to do a more thorough and formal assessment of your style, you'll want to order *The Gregorc Adult Style Delineator,*[1] available directly from Dr. Gregorc. And once again, keep in mind that all of us are combinations of these four learning styles. No person will fit totally into any one category.

Dominant Learning Style Characteristics

Describe what you prefer *most of the time*. Place a check mark beside every phrase under each section that describes your preferences. Check as many as you feel *strongly* describe you. The category you score the highest in is your dominant learning style.

Dominant Concrete Sequential (CS)

I almost always

___prefer doing things the same way

___work best with people who won't hesitate to take immediate action

___am more interested in obvious facts than in finding hidden meanings

___prefer a neat and orderly environment

___ask first "How do I do it?"

Total:____

Dominant Abstract Sequential (AS)

I almost always

___want as much information as possible before making a decision

___need enough time to do a thorough job

___prefer to get directions in writing

___am interested in where a person got the facts

___ask "Where do I find more information?"

Total:____

Dominant Abstract Random (AR)

I almost always

___prefer to check with others before making final decisions

___try to be sensitive to other people's feelings

___work well with others

___am not bothered by a cluttered environment

___ask the advice of others when in doubt

Total:____

Dominant Concrete Random (CR)

I almost always

___solve problems creatively

___act on the spur of the moment

___work best with those who can keep up

___like frequent changes in the environment

___prefer to learn only what's necessary to know

Total:____

Based on the work of Anthony F. Gregorc, Ph.D. Adapted by Cynthia Ulrich Tobias, M.Ed.
(Do not reproduce without written permission)

A professional young woman came up to me after a recent seminar and posed an interesting problem. She said she worked in the executive offices of a prestigious university. Although she had fielded hundreds of complex problems over the years, something she had never been able to figure out had to do with the office copy machine.

"It's not just that the whole office is paralyzed when the machine goes down," she explained, "it's that I've never been able to design the right out-of-order sign to keep everyone's hands off the machine until the repairman comes. Do you think this has anything to do with learning style?"

Her question intrigued me, and I began to design individually tailored out-of-order signs for each of the dominant Gregorc learning styles. The one for the Concrete Sequentials was easy:

OUT OF ORDER

My first version said OUT OF ORDER: DO NOT USE, but my CS friends and colleagues told me that was redundant. If the sign said out of order, they would not use it. So I dropped the second half and kept it simple.

The Abstract Sequential version was a little more difficult, so I turned to my AS husband for input. After careful deliberation, he came up with this:

OUT OF ORDER
Laymen's Options Have Been Exhausted; Expert Has Been Called

The sign for the Abstract Randoms was easily constructed:

> ## DO NOT DISTURB
> ### Machine Is Sick; Help Is on the Way

I really hit a brick wall when I got to the Concrete Randoms' sign. What would keep a strong-willed, adventurous, intuitive CR away from such an irresistible challenge as trying to heroically bring a vital piece of machinery back to life? I called some of my most trusted CR cohorts, but none of us could come up with the definitive sign. Finally, I thought of something that at least had a chance of success. One of the things we CRs hate most is being predictable. (We loathe hearing, "I knew you were going to do that.") So here's the sign:

And the CR's response should be, "Will not! Can't make me!"

> ## OUT OF ORDER
> ### (But You'll Probably Try It Anyway)

How do you get people to keep their hands off the copy machine (or any machine) that is out of order? Here are some suggestions for the various learning styles:

For the Dominant
Concrete Sequential

For the Dominant
Abstract Sequential

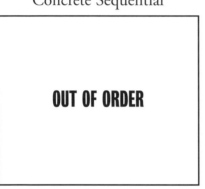

OUT OF ORDER

OUT OF ORDER

**Laymen's Options Have
Been Exhausted;
Expert Has Been Called**

For the Dominant
Abstract Random

For the Dominant
Concrete Random

DO NOT DISTURB

**Machine Is Sick
Help Is on the Way**

OUT OF ORDER

**(But You'll Probably
Try It Anyway)**

*Based on the work of Anthony F. Gregorc, Ph.D. Adapted by Cynthia Ulrich Tobias, M.Ed.
(Do not reproduce without written permission.)*

IN A NUTSHELL

Just because a person isn't responding to you doesn't necessarily mean he or she isn't listening. It could be that the difference in your perspectives is so great that you might as well be living in different countries and speaking different languages. Learning to listen to *how* something is said instead of just the *words* that are used can help everyone communicate more effectively. It can literally make a world of difference!

Chapter *Three*
THE DOMINANT CONCRETE SEQUENTIAL LEARNING STYLE

It was board meeting night for the local church. For some reason, those who attended that particular meeting preferred a more random style of learning and communicating. Missing were those with a Concrete Sequential (CS) learning style—those who approach tasks in a step-by-step manner. Since there was still a quorum, the randoms decided to go ahead with the meeting.

The main item on the agenda was promotion of an upcoming rally. "Hey!" someone said excitedly. "I've got a great idea!" (That phrase strikes dread in most CS hearts!) "What if we bought a thousand balloons and filled them with helium? We could put a notice about the rally inside each balloon and release them into the sky. They would come down all over the area, and people would find out about the event." All the other randoms thought that was a wonderful suggestion, and later that week, one of them went out and bought the balloons.

Before the actual launching of the balloons, however, there was one more board meeting, and the CS members showed up that night. The randoms enthusiastically described their plan, and the CSs politely listened. At the end, one CS raised his hand. "Do you know how far helium balloons go before they come down?" he asked.

The randoms looked a bit uncomfortable. "Well, no," one admitted.

The CS replied, "They've been known to go as far as two or three hundred miles. I don't think people on the other side of the mountains will come."

"Oh, yeah, we didn't think of that," a random said.

Another CS raised her hand. "Do you know how long helium balloons stay in the air before they come down?" she inquired.

"No," a random admitted, now a bit sheepish.

"They've been known to stay up as long as two or three months," the CS continued. "The rally will be over by then."

And the randoms said quietly, "Oh, yeah, you're right."

The box of one thousand balloons still sits, unused, under an office desk. But the board members learned a valuable lesson. In times past, the randoms had sometimes thought that the CSs were just shooting down good ideas and critically picking apart visionary plans. Now they realized that the CSs' contributions were invaluable. These days at that church's board meetings, it's not unusual to hear someone say, "Wait! We can't start without the CSs!"

THE DOMINANT CONCRETE SEQUENTIAL

When presented with an abstract idea, Concrete Sequentials have a special talent for seeing the practical side of it. They have a knack for knowing how to get the most productive use out of any item or plan for streamlining, and they can make everything work more efficiently. Their natural ability to think in a linear manner means they can actually put together those "ready to assemble" products by following the step-by-step instructions.

A CS lives in a fairly straightforward manner. Verbal communication sometimes comes across as clipped and bossy. The CS attitude is "If it needs to be done, you do it" and "If it needs to be said, you say it." CSs are no-nonsense communicators, saying what they mean and meaning what they say. They don't usually pick up on subtle clues or hidden meanings. They prefer you tell them exactly what you want them to do.

Although my husband is dominantly Abstract Sequential, he's also very CS. I learned long ago that when he uses his CS style, he needs more than hints to fulfill my wish list for gifts on special occasions. For our first Christmas together, he really built up his "big gift" to me. "It's red," he said, "something you'd never buy for yourself, and it's too big to fit under the tree." On Christmas Day, I found my gift sitting in the carport. It was a bright, shiny . . . lawn mower!

After a few more Christmases of receiving jumper cables, blenders, and shower curtains, I finally came to grips with the fact that he couldn't read my mind. He would keep telling me that he truly wanted to make me happy—but I needed to tell him what would make me happy. Although he's getting better at remembering what I like, he's absolutely thrilled when I just make him a list of exactly what I want.

Giving practical gifts is only one way dominant CSs demonstrate their ability for being down-to-earth and realistic. Because of their hands-on nature, they're very good at making and keeping schedules and organizing and maintaining systems. List-making comes naturally, and some extreme CSs even admit to being so dependent on a list that if they do something not on the list, they add it so they can have the satisfaction of crossing it off. CSs are often the ones taking up the slack, picking up the pieces, cleaning up the messes, and putting away the leftovers. CSs would rather do it themselves than leave it undone, but if they do it, they don't suffer silently! Those who live with CSs may find notes reminding them of their responsibilities, or they may receive quick lectures designed to leave them feeling at least a little guilty.

Dominant CSs have a definite sense of order and responsibility. They need to have a beginning, a middle, and an end.

The bleary-eyed couple was almost an hour late to a Saturday-morning workshop. The woman was very apologetic: "I'm afraid we overslept. We rented the three most boring movies last night. It took us until almost 2:00 A.M. to finish watching them."

When I asked why they had subjected themselves to such an endlessly boring evening, she looked surprised. "Why, we rented the movies," she said. "We started them. We couldn't just quit in the middle!"

THE DOMINANT CONCRETE SEQUENTIAL BOSS

When dealing with their employees, it's common for CS bosses to:

- Communicate in a literal, specific manner and expect the same in return.

- Believe that a yes or no question deserves a yes or no response, not a lengthy explanation.

- Expect instructions to be followed without question or procrastination.

- Clearly lay out the rules employees are expected to follow, as well as the consequences for noncompliance. Both are specific and consistent.

- Become frustrated when they have to say things more than once.

- Become exasperated at the person who seems to choose the "hard way" to do what the CS sees as a simple task.

CS employers almost always have high expectations when it comes to their employees' behavior and success. After all, the CS boss probably had little trouble adapting to the traditional methods used in management, since those methods tend to be concrete and sequential. If an employee is struggling, the CS boss may often believe it's because that employee is simply not trying hard enough.

CS bosses are not likely to accept excuses like "I don't know what you mean," "I don't understand," or "It doesn't make sense to me." Part of the CS nature is simply to do what needs to be done whether or not you understand it. Duty and obligation play a big part in their own lives, and they expect their employees to respond in the same way.

When it comes to discipline, CS bosses expect employees to do what they're told or suffer the consequences. In the CS mind, the threat of punishment should be enough to prevent incompetent or insubordinate behavior.

For an employee who is also Concrete Sequential, the CS boss's methods and approach make sense almost automatically. After all, they understand how each other's minds work. The CS employee finds it comforting to know what to expect, and there's a sense of security about the consistency of routine and schedule. For the more random employee, however, the CS boss's approach often seems dictatorial and rigid. Because a random person's perspective is so drastically different from a sequential's, trying to understand each other's point of view may literally be like listening to a foreign language.

THE DOMINANT CONCRETE SEQUENTIAL EMPLOYEE

The Concrete Sequential secretary had one of the company's most important clients on hold as she turned to her random boss. "What shall I tell him?" she asked.

Her boss was preoccupied. "I don't know," the boss said. "Just tell him whatever will make him happy."

The secretary looked puzzled for a moment. She shrugged, then spoke into the telephone. "We'll be glad to discount that order for you," she assured the client.

After she hung up, as her boss was loudly protesting, she replied, "But you said, 'Tell him what will make him happy.'"

That's a classic case of two different learning styles attempting to communicate. When it comes to dealing with a Concrete Sequential employee, a random employer must realize that the CS cannot read minds.

Some common characteristics of CS employees:
- They're usually very organized, specific, and conscientious.
- They may ask repeatedly for clarification or more-detailed

instructions because of their need to be sure they're doing things right.

- They're almost always more secure when there's a pattern to follow, a model to copy, or someone to go first and show them how it's done.

- In getting them to do their jobs, they respond best to tangible rewards and hands-on methods. A schedule or checklist can be a great motivator, especially for new employees.

- Consistency is especially important, and CS employees may frequently have to remind their more random bosses of appointments or missed steps in the routine. It may not even occur to the random bosses to create a checklist, much less keep it up to date!

- CS employees will generally take their bosses at their word. Since CSs tend to be very literal in their communication, more abstract employers may find their instructions misunderstood because they assumed the CS understood what was meant, not just what was said.

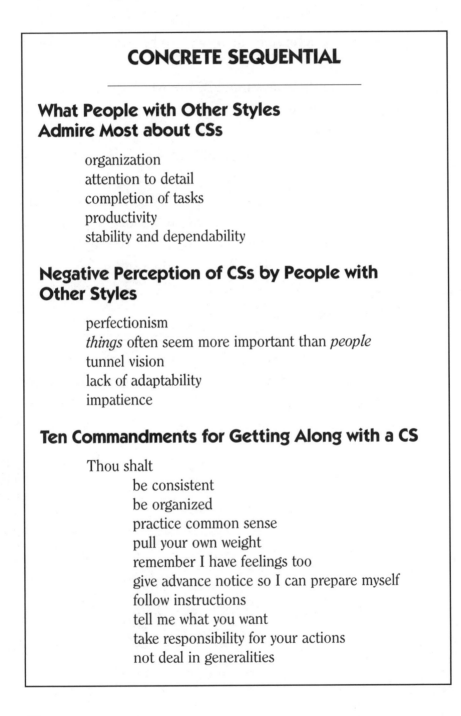

CONCRETE SEQUENTIAL

What People with Other Styles Admire Most about CSs

organization
attention to detail
completion of tasks
productivity
stability and dependability

Negative Perception of CSs by People with Other Styles

perfectionism
things often seem more important than *people*
tunnel vision
lack of adaptability
impatience

Ten Commandments for Getting Along with a CS

Thou shalt
be consistent
be organized
practice common sense
pull your own weight
remember I have feelings too
give advance notice so I can prepare myself
follow instructions
tell me what you want
take responsibility for your actions
not deal in generalities

How Do We Recognize . . .

The Dominant Concrete Sequential Customers

ORGANIZED

Did they schedule the visit in advance?
Do they automatically keep receipts or an auto log book?
Can they quickly locate keys, checkbook, credit cards?

DETAILED

Do they ask very specific questions?
Do they ask you to write down the information?
Do they often ask you to clarify what was said?

Based on the reseach of Anthony F. Gregorc, Ph.D. Terms used with permission.
Adapted by Cynthia Ulrich Tobias, M.Ed. Learning Styles Unlimited, Inc.
P.O. Box 1450, Sumner, WA 98390, (253) 862-6200

IN A NUTSHELL

Dominant Concrete Sequentials contribute a great deal to their jobs and society with their natural bent toward organization, predictability, literal communication, and following and giving step-by-step instructions. Their greatest creativity may show up when they're fine-tuning and improving another person's original idea. They provide a stable backdrop in the lives of those who may not even realize how much they count on having them there. Their consistency and reliability often make them more valuable than some randoms would like to admit. Remember that everyone has at least some of the CS style. Just because it isn't your dominant learning style doesn't mean you can't use it at least briefly when necessary. The more you learn to recognize CS strengths, the more you'll appreciate those who come by them naturally.

Chapter **Four**

THE DOMINANT ABSTRACT SEQUENTIAL LEARNING STYLE

I have always loved buying cars. During my years as a single person, I often traded cars every two years or so just for the sake of variety. I didn't even need to drive a car to know I should buy it; I would just intuitively know a particular car and I were meant for each other. My cars were personal friends. My Mitsubishi was Mitsi; my Monte Carlo (he had a drinking problem when it came to gas consumption) was Monty. And then I married my Abstract Sequential husband.

It was still early in our marriage when we discovered we needed to replace one of our cars. Acting in my typically random fashion, I said enthusiastically, "Let's go to the car lot and look around!"

My husband was incredulous. "We don't even know what we're looking *for*," he stated.

I shrugged and replied, "Won't we know when we see it?"

Three weeks later, after we had listed critical attributes, researched *Consumer Reports,* charted interest rates and lease options, and test-driven the top ten cars twice, I realized my car-buying days were changed forever. Although my AS husband took all the *romance* out of car shopping, we *did* make a significantly more economical choice.

THE DOMINANT ABSTRACT SEQUENTIAL

One of the greatest gifts the AS possesses is *objectivity.* ASs, by their very nature, will check out all the possibilities, look at all the angles, and carefully weigh all the evidence before making a decision. ASs may enjoy being entertained by snappy commercials, but don't kid yourself—serious purchases will not be made lightly. The process of gathering information is so important to ASs that they don't do much of anything without a great deal of deliberation. They analytically evaluate virtually everything, from major decisions to a simple lunch choice on a restaurant menu.

What's especially unique about the AS evaluation process is that the analysis doesn't stop even after the final decision has been made. Although the process is done less actively, ASs admit they never really stop looking to make sure there isn't a better option.

If an item has already been purchased and ASs later find a better deal, there are, for them, really only two choices. If it's not too late, the item is exchanged. If it *is* too late, ASs may kick themselves for years, and there's almost nothing you can do to lessen the remorse.

Even though this may sound extreme, I've been told by several ASs that their penchant for finding the absolute best bargain even extends to the gifts they receive. As they are opening their gifts, the most dominant ASs can't resist calculating how they could get *twice* the merchandise for the exchange value of the gift if they just waited for the right sale.

Analysis comes naturally to ASs, and most believe there can *never* really be enough information. They seem to be on a continual search for knowledge. There aren't enough hours in each day for ASs to do the research they feel is needed.

Since most ASs assume everyone has their same need for extensive information, you may frequently get long answers to short questions. It's difficult for ASs not to monopolize a conversation when the topic interests them. And even though you may be finished listening, they may not pick up on your impatience.

The need for analysis and objectivity carries over into the more personal aspects of AS lives. Although ASs may experience as much emotion as the next person, they believe their emotions should be justified by facts. For example, I'm told by many ASs that falling in love is a difficult situation when it comes to applying principles of logic and reason. Most ASs may revel in the euphoric emotion of love, but they rarely make a serious commitment until they are certain there are solid and reliable facts to back up their emotional involvement. ASs will rarely express what they're feeling until they have a handle on *why* they're feeling the way they do. By the same token, they expect you to be able to justify *your* emotions.

I learned some important lessons about ASs early in my relationship with the man who is now my husband. We had only been dating about three months when we had a pretty serious argument. I was so upset when we parted that I went right home and poured my jumbled thoughts out on paper, not sure if I actually dared to send the letter to John. After some soul-searching, I went ahead and mailed it.

A day or so later, John called me and asked if he could take me to lunch to discuss my letter. He picked me up, and while we were sitting in the car, he took out my heartfelt, soul-baring epistle. He had rewritten it in outline form—Roman numerals I, II, III; subheads A, B, C. I was too horrified to speak! He sensed my dismay and quickly explained. "Cindy, I love you," he said. "What you wrote obviously meant a lot to you. If I were to just answer you off the top of my head, I might well miss the points that were most important to you. So I put this in a format where I could be sure all your concerns were addressed."

How could I argue with that? His meticulous approach that at first seemed to be so cold and calculating was actually motivated by the same love and tenderness that had caused me to randomly spill my thoughts onto paper.

THE DOMINANT ABSTRACT SEQUENTIAL BOSS

AS bosses insist that their employees demonstrate at least some semblance of logical thought and analysis. Because of a naturally intellectual bent, AS bosses can sometimes unintentionally make their more random employees feel intellectually inferior. AS employers tend to have high expectations for their departments.

Remember, ASs believe in thorough deliberation and complete analysis of virtually every situation. A simple request from an employee like "Could we put a vending machine in the employee lounge?" may well bring about more trouble than that employee thinks it's worth! The AS boss will likely respond with questions like "What kind of machine? Where will you put it? How will you stock it? Who will maintain it? How much will it cost? Where does the profit go, and how will it be calculated?" AS bosses will likely require their employees to keep detailed records or present a well-thought-out written request in the first place.

It's especially important to AS employers that their employees learn to think logically. ASs feel compelled to look beyond the obvious and find the underlying principle. This understanding of the "moral of the story" often creates the need for an AS boss to be sure everyone has "learned his lesson." ASs have a strong need for closure, and they often find themselves asking, "Now, what have you learned from this?" An employee with a random style may create a great deal of frustration for the AS boss, because it seems almost impossible to direct that dominantly random mind into a structured analysis of circumstances or problems.

A visiting professor recently told me her AS husband was fond of lecturing their impatient and impetuous teenage daughter. The girl hated the long, drawn-out lectures, and her father was very annoyed by her obvious lack of attention. After several mutually frustrating encounters, they came up with an agreement. When the father started to lecture, the daughter could stop him at any time and state the point she thought he was trying to make. If she got it right, he had to abort the rest of the lecture. If she missed the point, he was allowed to continue until she understood. Now he knew she was listening, and she knew she wouldn't need to endure a prolonged explanation of a point he had already driven home.

That's the kind of compromise that can help AS employers come to terms with those who don't share their drive to analyze, verbalize, and philosophize.

THE DOMINANT ABSTRACT SEQUENTIAL EMPLOYEE

Here are some common characteristics of Abstract Sequential employees:

- They're systematic and deliberate.
- They almost always need more time to complete tasks to their satisfaction.
- They would rather not do an assignment or project at all if there isn't time to do it completely.
- They may appear quiet and withdrawn.
- They won't usually verbalize what they're thinking until they understand it.

One extroverted boss became worried about her uncommunicative AS assistant, Angela. Although very efficient, Angela spent hours alone in her office without talking or interacting with other staff members. Angela's written work, however, was superb. Her employer attended one of my workshops on learning styles and discovered Angela's AS strengths. After coming to understand the AS approach, this normally outspoken boss was able to keep silent and appreciate the depth of insight Angela possessed. When the boss let her AS colleague work in solitude without pressure, Angela began to be more comfortable verbalizing what she was doing, and soon she started interacting with other staff members.

Because of ASs' need for objectivity, they're often uncomfortable with tasks or projects that seem too personal. It's difficult for them to express emotions, especially if the emotions can't be explained logically or categorized efficiently. If you're working with an AS who seems to be struggling with this, you may be able to help by encouraging an analysis of why something is happening instead of focusing on the personal effects.

ABSTRACT SEQUENTIAL

What People with Other Styles Admire Most about ASs

ability to analyze before making a decision
talent for conceptualizing an idea
intellect
precision
ready knowledge

Negative Perceptions of ASs by People with Other Styles

aloof
not in touch with reality
have to have an explanation for everything
highly opinionated
perceive things in numbers, not effort

Ten Commandments for Getting Along with an AS

Thou shalt

have specific goals when dealing with me
use logic and reason
listen to what I have to say
give me a job, leave me alone, and let me do it
be complete and thorough
be deliberate
keep issues factual
give me time to research projects for the best approach
make certain I understand the purpose of the project
not expect an immediate response—I need time to
        think and research

How Do We Recognize . . .

The Dominant Abstract Sequential Customers

THOROUGH

Do they insist on a full explanation?
Do they usually want more information than most?
Do they debate the options before making a decision?

DELIBERATE

Are they slow to make a decision?
Do they actually read the brochures you give them?
Do they usually shop around before deciding on you?

Based on the reseach of Anthony F. Gregorc, Ph.D. Terms used with permission.
Adapted by Cynthia Ulrich Tobias, M.Ed. Learning Styles Unlimited, Inc.
P.O. Box 1450, Sumner, WA 98390, (253) 862-6200

IN A NUTSHELL

The dominant AS is in the minority among the general population. The views of the strong AS will not always make sense to, or even be welcomed by, those who don't share the same devotion to logic and objectivity. Although it may seem that the AS has an entirely too serious and methodical perspective on life, there's also a warm and loving side that can sometimes be overlooked by those who don't recognize or value the AS's approach. Once again, we all have at least a little of every learning style. Even if your AS tendencies are virtually hidden, learning how to access this part of your style can definitely be a benefit.

Chapter Five
THE DOMINANT ABSTRACT RANDOM LEARNING STYLE

The suspect in the crime sat alone in the interrogation room. Officer Baker, one of the department's best by-the-book cops, had stormed out in frustration. "He won't talk!" Baker growled. "I tried every method we were ever taught, and the guy won't budge."

Detective Frye smiled and said, "Let me talk to him."

"I'm telling you," Baker said angrily, "I've tried it all."

Detective Frye had been in the room less than five minutes when Baker, watching the suspect through the one-way mirror, stared in disbelief. The suspect's head was in his hands, and he was sobbing. Detective Frye had turned on the recorder, and the full confession took less than an hour.

"What did you do?" Baker asked when Frye came out.

Detective Frye shrugged and said, "I just talked to him."

THE DOMINANT ABSTRACT RANDOM

During my time as a police officer, I noticed that dominantly sequential officers had a particularly frustrating time dealing with unpredictable or uncooperative people. In the police academy, we were taught how to interrogate a suspect, interview a victim, and solicit information from a witness. There are certain procedures to follow. So when a sequential officer follows procedure to the letter and those tried-and-true methods fail, he or she is often at a loss. That's what happened in the preceding story. Officer Baker, a CS, could not understand how Detective Frye, an AR, could come in, speak a couple of sentences, and cause the suspect to pour out his heart. But in many cases, the technique simply isn't something one could learn from a book.

For the past few years, the corporate world has shown a strong interest in "intuitive management." Instead of automatically valuing a management style that relies solely on straightforward facts and logic, our increasingly service-oriented society realizes the need for a more flexible approach. Usually those with the dominantly sequential learning styles can quickly be taught the traditional management methods. But they often struggle when it comes to adapting to an approach that relies on a less definitive, more intuitive ability to "read" and understand people.

The AR has a sixth sense when it comes to reading between the lines or understanding what others need, even those who can't verbalize their needs. Nonverbal cues that may completely escape the more sequential person can speak volumes to the AR. Because ARs place so much trust in intuition, their instincts become more and more accurate over the years. It's not any easier for ARs to explain *how* they know what they know, however, if they didn't use sequential abilities in arriving at their conclusions.

Dominant Abstract Random people believe there's more to life than cold, hard facts or endless details. People are more important than things, and life is too short to get caught up in conflict or uncomfortable situations. They often find themselves the peacemakers, sometimes at their own expense. It's difficult for ARs to work in situations where there's unhappiness or disharmony. For many ARs, it seems as though they're constantly having to smooth over rough words said by someone else or to apologize for the actions of a thoughtless colleague or family member.

It's especially important for ARs to feel included. Before making a decision, they almost always seek the input of trusted friends and family. ARs are at their best when they're part of a team process. Soliciting opinions from those around them helps them maintain a cooperative lifestyle.

Although my dominant style is Concrete Random, my AR preferences are very strong. I noticed how heavily I relied on my AR side early in my dating relationship with my very sequential husband, when we would experience a conflict common to many couples.

John would ask, "Do you want to go out for dinner?"

"Yes," I would reply enthusiastically.

"Where would you like to go?" he would query.

Not wanting to make an unpopular choice, I would hedge. "I don't know. What do *you* feel like eating?"

He would shrug. "It doesn't matter. Just choose a restaurant."

Not actually *believing* it didn't matter, I would keep after him until he became impatient with me. Why couldn't I just make a *decision*? I would feel hurt. Didn't he realize it was because I valued his opinion? Of course, by the time we finally *did* get to a restaurant, we were too irritated with each other to enjoy our dinner.

Eventually we both realized what the other person needed, so John then designed an almost foolproof method for avoiding the conflict. Now when the question of where to go for dinner comes up, he says, "Chinese, Mexican, or American?" He chooses three cuisines he would be equally happy eating.

"Chinese," I say.

He then suggests three Chinese restaurants he finds equally appealing. I choose one of those three, and we're off, usually in less than a minute. I get the necessary input, he gets a quick decision, and we both enjoy our evening!

What may seem to others to be a lack of conviction or inability to make up their minds is often simply the AR's effort to make sure that everyone involved in the process gets what he or she needs. In reality, ARs often possess the strongest convictions of all, and once they've chosen their priorities, no one is more committed to the end result.

THE ABSTRACT RANDOM BOSS

The AR boss's office was happily chaotic, with piles of papers, a half-empty coffee cup, and stacks of files. Almost hidden on the desk was a lovingly framed sign declaring a cheerful AR motto: "A clean desk is the sign of a sick mind!"

Although ARs can keep their offices clean as well as any sequential, housekeeping is not a high priority if there are personal needs to fulfill. By nature, ARs are somewhat unstructured and free-flowing, and they often struggle when it comes to keeping a consistent schedule or detailed routine. Dominantly AR employers are warm, nurturing, and full of praise and reassurance for their team. A more sequential employee may perceive an AR boss as inconsistent, even though it may simply be a case of deciding what really needs to be an issue and what isn't all that important.

The ARs' avoidance of conflict can sometimes make them a target for being the "soft touch." In many cases, ARs would simply rather "switch than fight." They do strive to maintain harmony, and that can mean giving in on issues that may have been firmly enforced by their more sequential counterparts. Although ARs will usually stand firm for the nonnegotiable issues of physical safety and moral and ethical values, almost everything else is really dependent on the day and the mood of the AR. Unfortunately, this may send mixed messages, especially to a more sequential employee, who may get in trouble for doing something one day and the next day have it go by completely unnoticed.

ARs are usually very conscientious supervisors, and they often feel bad that they are asking their employees to be organized and tidy when they themselves are hard-pressed to do the same. It's relatively easy to make ARs feel guilty. Early in the working relationship, employees pick up on this and can soon be manipulating the AR boss. ARs are very sensitive to how others feel, and it is both an asset and a liability to care so much about what others think.

THE ABSTRACT RANDOM EMPLOYEE

The dominant Abstract Random, probably more than any of the other learning styles, cares about pleasing people. Here are some common characteristics of dominant AR employees:

- All of life and learning is an intensely personal experience.
- They find it difficult to work on something that doesn't have any effect on their own lives or the lives of those who matter to them.
- They may be accused frequently of "not living up to your potential" because they rarely pursue knowledge purely for the love of learning.
- They have a difficult time working when others aren't happy.
- They tend to be highly sensitive to strife between colleagues.

Although ARs aren't usually perceived as extremely intellectual, they possess as much intelligence as people with any other learning style. There is, however, a catch. ARs don't choose to use their intelligence in situations that don't interest them personally.

In the nursing program at a local university, administrators discovered they were losing a lot of potentially good nursing candidates. On closer examination, they found that many of the dropouts were AR students. The ARs were drawn to the profession out of a sense of personal nurturing and devotion to the well-being of others. Unfortunately, no one had really warned them about all the very *un*-AR classes that must be endured before they could fulfill their dream.

The professors decided to stay close to the AR students and regularly remind them why they had wanted to become nurses in the first place—to save lives and make a difference. Somehow it made the classes in physics, chemistry, and anatomy into personal challenges that must be met to achieve the ultimate goal. Almost everyone discovered that the AR can ace the most difficult class as long as there's a personal, passionate commitment to the outcome.

Because ARs have a "sixth sense" about what people need, they're often the first to point out a problem with staff morale. It's as if they have an invisible antenna up at all times, scanning the atmosphere for trouble spots. Others in the office are often drawn to ARs as sounding boards, confidants, and friends. But it may be difficult to get AR employees to focus on facts and logic when they're much more acutely aware of feelings and relationships.

ABSTRACT RANDOM

What People with Other Styles Admire Most about ARs

spontaneity

concern for others

sociability

adaptability

ability to understand
how others feel

Negative Perceptions of ARs by People with Other Styles

unpredictable

don't take a hard stand

overly sensitive to criticism

not aware of time limitations

smooth over problems rather than solve them

Ten Commandments for Getting Along with ARs

Thou shalt

give me the opportunity to help others

give me feedback (positive/negative)—where do I stand?

not be so serious

not nitpick

realize that I will get things done—even if it's not your way

not put me in the middle of a conflict

allow me to be spontaneous

show appreciation

not mistake a happy exterior for lack of intelligence

know that not all is written in stone

How Do We Recognize . . .

The Dominant Abstract Random Customers

PERCEPTIVE

Do they seem concerned about you personally?
Can they usually tell what mood you're in?
Do they often read more into what you say?

COOPERATIVE

Do they want your personal opinion?
Do they ask what you would do if you were them?
Do they try to make things convenient for you?

Based on the reseach of Anthony F. Gregorc, Ph.D. Terms used with permission.
Adapted by Cynthia Ulrich Tobias, M.Ed. Learning Styles Unlimited, Inc.
P.O. Box 1450, Sumner, WA 98390, (253) 862-6200

IN A NUTSHELL

When it comes to being in touch with others, sensing what needs to be done, and getting along with difficult people, there aren't any better candidates for sainthood than ARs. As one person put it, "When they gave out love and kindness, you ARs got double-dipped!" Other styles can sometimes sell the ARs short by not appreciating the spontaneity and flexibility that come as part of the package. If we want to get along with other people, we must all use our AR skills daily.

Chapter *Six*
THE DOMINANT CONCRETE RANDOM LEARNING STYLE

They were sitting in the lunchroom, and the Concrete Sequential had just taken a big drink of juice when she made a horrible face and spit it out. "Ack! This tastes awful!" she said.

Her Concrete Random colleague reached for the glass. "Let me try it," he offered.

She looked at him as if he had lost his mind. "Don't you trust me?" she asked. "Why would you want to taste something I just told you was awful?"

It wasn't that her CR colleague didn't trust her—he just needed to experience bad-tasting juice in order to believe it actually tasted bad, just as he needed to experience all facts in order to believe them.

THE DOMINANT CONCRETE RANDOM

Because the CR lives in the "real world," usually anything that can't be experienced firsthand cannot be fully trusted. CRs are notorious risk takers. They believe you can't break away from the ordinary unless you're willing to go out on a limb.

Dominant CR people are probably the least likely to take your word about anything. They have a compelling need to try things for themselves. CRs, more than any other style, strive not to be ordinary. If you say a rule or plan is for everyone, CRs will tell you they are not everyone, so what's true for others isn't necessarily true for them.

CRs are intuitive, quick-thinking, curious, and resourceful. The concrete part of their nature makes them very hands-on, but their random ordering process causes them to be somewhat unpredictable. The CRs often fight structure and routine, preferring to keep all their options open. Life usually goes by at a breathless pace with them because they're constantly looking for new challenges and untried doors. If something becomes routine or boring, CRs simply drop it and go on to the next, more exciting prospect.

It's not unusual for CRs to have several careers in a lifetime, sometimes even two careers at once. That doesn't reflect a lack of focus as much as a desire for variety, a sense of being able to conquer the unknown. The resourceful CR nature keenly grasps the obvious and can quickly turn it into something unexpected.

As I was driving home the other evening, I heard my two-and-a-half-year-old twin sons arguing in the backseat. Michael (CR extraordinaire) was hitting his AR brother, Robert. Although I suspected what was going on, I decided to give Michael the benefit of the doubt.

"Michael," I said sternly, "I'm pulling over and turning on the light. If you're hitting your brother, you're in big trouble."

I stopped the car, switched on the light, and turned around to see Michael's hand resting on his brother's arm. With lightning-fast thinking, Mike grinned at me and said, "Tickle, tickle, tickle!"

It was a perfect example of the CR's natural gift for getting in and out of trouble quickly. Because they can think so well on their feet, it's rare that you can catch them violating a given rule, even if they get off on a technicality.

CRs, for the most part, consider most rules to be simply guidelines. In their thinking, rules are for people who don't know how to do the right thing in the first place.

I am, admittedly, a strong CR. One year it was almost Christmas, and my AR sister Sandee, one of her small children, and I were shopping in a department store. When we got to the escalator with the stroller, Sandee noticed a sign that said, "No strollers allowed on the escalator." While she was reading the sign, I was busy loading the stroller onto the moving stairway.

Sandee was horrified. "The sign says no strollers on the escalator!" she cried.

I looked at her. "Oh, are the stroller police going to get us?" I asked sarcastically. "Sandee, this sign is for people who don't know how to safely put a stroller on an escalator. Since I do know how, it doesn't apply to me."

She refused to follow me upstairs for several minutes, not wanting anyone in the store to realize she was with someone who so blatantly disregarded a rule. For me, it was simply a guideline.

A few months ago, I was walking through a busy airport. As I approached the escalators, I noticed a young couple coming up the escalator with a huge baby buggy. Even at a distance, I could see the wife was really upset with her husband. As I passed them, I heard him tell her, "Nobody died. Did anybody die? Nobody died!"

It's difficult for the CR to accept limits and restrictions, especially if the rules seem arbitrary or dictatorial. Most CRs believe in being law-abiding citizens and are especially conscious of setting a good example for their children. But CRs have the most trouble with regulations that don't seem to have a practical reason for their existence.

"Rank has its privileges" is not a CR motto, and "Just because I said so" is almost never accepted without challenge. The CR will not be deterred by the word "impossible" if he or she has determined the goal is worthy. At the other extreme, even the most accessible goal may be ignored by a CR who has decided that achieving it just isn't worth the trouble.

One young CR woman came up after a recent seminar and said, "I just have to tell you my own CR story!" She said that when she enrolled in a college chemistry class, she was surprised to hear the professor make a rather brash statement at the beginning of the first session. He told the students that since no one could possibly get an A on any test without doing the homework, the homework would count as 50 percent of the total semester grade.

This CR woman immediately bristled. What did he mean it wasn't possible to get an A without doing the homework? "Right then and there," she told me, "I decided I wasn't going to do a drop of homework. And I did get an A on every test."

I smiled at her and said, "But you got a C in the class, didn't you?"

She grinned as she answered, "Yep, but it was the best C I ever got!"

CRs sometimes frustrate people of more sequential styles because they don't go by the book, and they constantly seek to change the system or try something new. It is these very bents, however, that keep everyone growing and challenged to consider new and uncharted possibilities.

THE DOMINANT CONCRETE RANDOM BOSS

Concrete Random employers often find themselves frustrated by CR employees who simply don't do as they're told. Now, mind you, CR bosses would be the last to do something just because you said so. But once CRs have decided how something should be, they tend to issue orders in a way that they themselves probably wouldn't respond to positively. It's something like the following classic struggle between a CR father and his CR son.

The young father read his four-year-old son a bedtime story and tucked him in. As the father left the room, the boy said, "Dad, leave the hall light on."

Dad replied, "No, son, we're not going to leave the hall light on."

"Yes, I want the hall light on."

"No, no hall light."

"Yes!"

"No!"

"Yes!"

"No!" And the hall light went off.

The boy started to cry. The parents decided he could jolly well cry himself to sleep. But two hours later, everybody was sick of it. The boy was tired of crying, but he wasn't going to give in. The parents were tired of listening to him, but it had been decided that the hall light was not going to go on.

Finally the father walked back down the hall, looked into the room, and discovered his son had uncovered one of his feet. The teary-eyed little boy said, "Dad, if you'll cover my foot, I'll go to sleep."

So his dad covered his foot, and the boy went to sleep. You see, the war was no longer worth winning—but for both CR parent and CR child, unconditional surrender was out of the question. The father needed to maintain his authority as a parent, but his compromise allowed his son a graceful way to surrender the battle.

CRs are passionate about their convictions. CRs want the best for their company, but they can sometimes find themselves insisting that their employees accept the CR way whether they like it or not. One of the greatest challenges for those working with the CR is often providing a graceful way for the CR to surrender.

CRs often make fun and exciting bosses, actively participating in almost everything and encouraging their colleagues to pursue the job for all they're worth. Life for CRs is an adventure, and they'll be the first to conquer uncharted territories and slay scary dragons. Often the CR boss emerges from his office and says, "Hey, I've got a great idea"—not even noticing how many sequential employees cringe at the thought of yet another new project or new direction.

Because CR employers understand the CR nature of their employees, you would think they would get along well. Although they sometimes do, being alike is not always a benefit. Since a CR boss doesn't want to back down any more than a CR employee does, it can create a standoff between the two.

THE DOMINANT CONCRETE RANDOM EMPLOYEE

Some common characteristics of dominant Concrete Random employees:

- They're usually full of energy, curiosity, and new ideas.
- Boredom is their greatest enemy.
- They would rather create a crisis than see a day go by without incident.
- They are determined to stay in control of their own lives.
- They expect to have some input into how rules are made and enforced.

CRs have a nature that resists ultimatums. If you say "Do this or else," CRs will most likely choose "else." They may do it quietly, without fuss, but CRs know there's nothing they really have to do except die (which, by the way, they're willing to do if necessary). People with most other styles are not willing to perish over the small things, but CRs are.

I had a successful career as a reserve police officer in a local municipality. I was actively and fully commissioned for almost six years, with an excellent record and commendations. I loved the job and got along well with my superiors, even though the police department is largely a paramilitary organization and very Concrete Sequential.

One day the lieutenant called me in and informed me there was to be a change in policy, and I would be required to cut my hair above the collar. Since I was one of only two women on the force, I questioned why I had to comply with the same hair standards set for the men. My lieutenant smiled and firmly said, "Because this is the new policy we have adopted."

I politely replied, "I understand that, but why do I need to change my hairstyle when the one I have is working just fine?"

My lieutenant started over. "Perhaps you didn't understand me when I said this is the new policy. The bottom line is, either you get your hair cut or you don't work."

I had no choice, no control, so I quietly and calmly quit. There are no hard feelings. In fact, I still teach classes for the department. But as a CR, I simply could not live with the ultimatum.

Although CR employees can easily exasperate their bosses, the fact is that CRs expect boundaries and actually welcome the security of knowing the limits. The greatest challenge is in the way an employer communicates authority and how much input the CR employee has to the rules and consequences.

The best way to explain it is with what I call my "drive-through theory." When I stop at the fast-food drive-through and give my order to the little box, I often hear something like, "That will be $3.86. Please drive forward." Isn't that a keen sense of the obvious? Do they think I'm too stupid to know I'm supposed to drive forward to the window? By the time I get to the cashier, I'm so irritated I never want to come back.

On the other hand, when I hear, "That will be $3.86 at the first window, please," I know exactly what I'm supposed to pay and where I'm supposed to go. And it's said in a way that assumes I'm a smart and capable person. Now, that may not seem like such a big deal to you, but to CRs, it's essential that you give them credit for knowing the right thing to do.

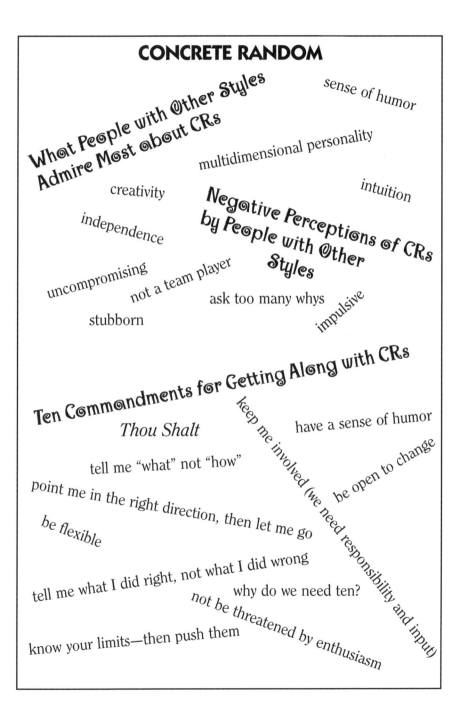

CONCRETE RANDOM

What People with Other Styles Admire Most about CRs

sense of humor

multidimensional personality

creativity

intuition

Negative Perceptions of CRs by People with Other Styles

independence

uncompromising

not a team player

ask too many whys

impulsive

stubborn

Ten Commandments for Getting Along with CRs

Thou Shalt

keep me involved (we need responsibility and input)

have a sense of humor

tell me "what" not "how"

be open to change

point me in the right direction, then let me go

be flexible

tell me what I did right, not what I did wrong

why do we need ten?

not be threatened by enthusiasm

know your limits—then push them

How Do We Recognize . . .

The Dominant Concrete Random Customers

CREATIVE

Do they want a lot of options?
Do they often look for unusual or less obvious solutions?
Do they seem drawn toward unique approaches?

SPONTANEOUS

Do they usually make decisions quickly?
Are they easily inspired to try something new?
Do they seem impatient with minor details?

Based on the reseach of Anthony F. Gregorc, Ph.D. Terms used with permission.
Adapted by Cynthia Ulrich Tobias, M.Ed. Learning Styles Unlimited, Inc.
P.O. Box 1450, Sumner, WA 98390, (253) 862-6200

Now that you have some understanding of learning styles and have, I hope, identified your own, you may find it helpful to take a piece of paper and draw a picture that illustrates some of the characteristics of your learning style. To get you started, here's a picture that represents the characteristics of an Abstract Random learning style. We're only using the AR style as an example. If you're a different learning style, your picture will look very different.

Save your picture. We'll be adding more learning style elements to it as we go along.

IN A NUTSHELL

When working with parents of strong-willed, CR children, I often tell them their kids are going to change the world. After all, it's not likely the world is going to change them. Once you begin to understand CR strengths, you'll be amazed to notice how much CRs contribute to keeping the world moving and growing. Instead of forcing CRs to conform, perhaps we should take more notice of how many of their ideas have real merit. The CR in all of us may just save us from ourselves!

Chapter Seven

HOW DO WE CONCENTRATE?

Now that you have a basic grasp of Gregorc's description of how our minds work, let me add another layer to the overall picture. We all have certain preferences for our most productive work environment. Such things as the way an office is lighted or heated, whether the chairs are comfortable, and whether we're hungry can all influence our ability to concentrate. Identifying these environmental preferences will add an important dimension to our understanding of learning styles.

The editorial office of one publisher I know offers more variety in environment and atmosphere than many I've seen. One desk is piled high with stacks of papers while the editor works at a clean table across the room. Another editor is quietly bent over his work, frowning while he tries to keep distractions from overtaking his concentration. In the far corner sits a friendly-looking round table with a living-room lamp instead of the glaring fluorescent lights. Nearest the door, although immersed in her work, an employee smiles and sways to the music coming through the headphones over her ears.

If we truly want employees to be as productive as possible, we need to let them identify and use their natural environmental preferences to help them concentrate and work. Let's look at some different work surroundings and see which are best.

Among the leading researchers in this field are the husband-and-wife team of Kenneth and Rita Dunn.[1] The Dunns have spent years studying the effects of environment on an individual and the individual's inborn learning style as it relates to concentrating and remembering information. (See the bibliography for more on this topic.) Using the Dunns' research, let me highlight a few important factors you should consider while trying to find the most effective way to help each person in your office concentrate.

WHERE SHOULD YOU WORK?

The traditional idea of a suitable place to work has been around for generations. The standard approach is to insist on a clean, quiet, well-lit room with a desk and chair. For many people, this is an effective way to concentrate. For some of us, however, it's tantamount to being imprisoned without possibility of parole.

I have always favored working on the floor, both as a student and as an adult. Even if I'm dressed in a business suit, I close my office door and spread everything out on the floor before commencing my work. At home, my husband will often find me hunched over books and papers on the floor, lost in thought. He is concerned.

"The light is terrible in here!" he exclaims. "And you're going to ruin your back sitting on the floor like that. Here, here! We have a perfectly clean and wonderful rolltop desk." He sweeps up my papers and neatly places them on the desk, helps me into the chair, turns on the high-intensity lamp, and pats my shoulder.

"Now, isn't that better?" he asks.

I smile and wait until he's down the hall and out of sight. Then I gather all my papers and go back to the floor. You see, I could sit at the rolltop desk for as long as he really needed me to sit there. But that's all I'd be doing—sitting at the rolltop desk. I could sit there for an hour, and when he came back I wouldn't have done anything.

"What's the matter?" he'd ask. "You've had ideal conditions: an hour of uninterrupted time and a clean, well-lit place to work. Why haven't you *done* anything?"

It doesn't occur to him that anyone in his or her right mind could actually work better on the floor than at the desk, or concentrate better in ten-minute spurts, with music or noise in the background, than in a silent sixty-minute block of time.

Sitting on the couch or curling up on the floor is the only way some people can be comfortable enough to really concentrate. Although some environments are simply not flexible enough to accommodate everyone, it's important to remember that even minor adjustments can greatly improve productivity.

HOW QUIET SHOULD IT BE?

You may have a hard time imagining that a person could actually *need* noise to keep from being distracted. I, for one, am greatly distracted by solitude and silence. My husband, on the other hand, is *dependent* on those two elements for any constructive task.

Many offices pipe in recorded music for everyone. Others allow for radios on individual desks. Still others insist on silence unless the employees want to wear headphones for listening to music. If you observe those around you, you'll notice how important it is for some to have absolute quiet, while others will try almost anything to introduce a little noise into the background.

WHAT ABOUT LIGHT?

As we were growing up, most of us heard our moms say, "Turn on the light, or you'll ruin your eyes!" The truth is, we all seem to have different levels of tolerance for bright or dim light. In most families, there's at least one person who goes around turning lights *off* behind the person who is turning every light *on*. Although many offices insist on using bright overhead fluorescent lights, some people may *lose* concentration because they need softer light.

If possible, experiment with different levels of light in order to find the one that's most comfortable and produces the best working environment for you. Perhaps you'll have to bring a lamp from home or add spot lighting to achieve a comfortable level in your office. Remember, the chances are good that *your* preference will be different from that of your colleague on the other side of the room.

SHOULD YOU TURN UP THE HEAT?

If you walk into almost any office building, you'll find some people sitting comfortably in lightweight, short-sleeved shirts while others are shivering in their sweaters or jackets. And if the temperature is too hot or too cold, many people will be unable to concentrate. While some adapt easily to varying temperatures, others need for the room to be at their comfort level before they can pay attention to anything else.

One of my favorite anecdotes was related during a workshop by Rita Dunn, the researcher I mentioned earlier. As she worked with young students who were learning English as a second language, she tried to test their knowledge of basic words. "What is a sweater?" she asked.

One small boy near the front immediately raised his hand and answered matter-of-factly, "It's what your mother makes you wear when she's cold."

SHOULD EMPLOYEES BE ALLOWED TO EAT ON THE JOB?

Many offices have had a long-standing rule that no food or drink is allowed except during break time, and even then it's consumed only in the lunch or break room. For some, that's not a problem, since eating or drinking might distract them from their work. For others, however, eating or drinking may actually be necessary to keep their minds focused on what they're doing. If you need a cup of coffee or can of soda handy while working, you probably understand why many are distracted if they must work when hungry or thirsty.

If you see a colleague chewing on a pencil or biting a fingernail, it could be that he or she is desperately trying not to think about the hunger pangs that are threatening to overshadow any productive activities. Although it's not always practical to have food and drink at the desk, often just a piece of hard candy or chewing gum is enough to help a hungry worker concentrate on what needs to be done instead of thinking about lunch.

LISTENING TO THE INTERNAL TIME CLOCK

Since I've always been a morning person, I was surprised to find out that some people are actually *annoyed* by those who appear too alert or cheerful before 10:00 A.M. On the other hand, I'm ready to call it a day before the eleven o'clock news, while the night people are just getting their greatest spurt of energy. Although we can discipline ourselves to cope at just about any time of day, most of us have certain hours when we're naturally more energetic.

If you have one person in the office who is most alert in the morning and another who's the proverbial night owl, it's unrealistic to expect them both to do their best job at the same time of day. It also stands to reason that when you must do a difficult or boring task, you'll do better if you can schedule it during your most alert time of day. If you can, your overall concentration will be greatly improved.

If at all possible, encourage your organization to consider the concept of *flextime*. Not only will employees be able to arrange their day to fit a schedule that's more convenient, but you may find that their productivity is sharply increased as well.

Note: It's important to remember that not all these categories of environmental preferences are equally important to all people. Certain factors may matter a great deal to some. Others may just be a bonus. For example, I concentrate better when I can eat or drink something while I'm working, but I *can* work without it. I can't work at *all* if I'm cold. Try to identify the elements that are absolutely essential to your ability to concentrate. Then work at achieving as many environmental preferences as possible, as often as possible.

If you're an employer, remember that employees should not use their learning styles as an excuse to avoid doing something they don't like. If you define the specific outcomes you want them to accomplish, you can help them achieve those outcomes in a way that makes the most sense to *their* natural learning styles. Then the chances for success and productivity will be much greater. In circumstances where you can't accommodate your employees' natural preferences, you can help them understand and cope with the demands of doing whatever they must by recognizing and then talking with them about their work environment.

PUTTING IT INTO ACTION

As an employer, the following suggestions can help you identify some of your employees' natural environmental preferences.

As you work through these suggestions, you may discover some of your own learning-style strengths as well. Discussing your preferences can help all of you understand your similarities and differences.

- Give all employees a large piece of paper and some markers. Ask them to draw a picture of the ideal work area. Ask for as many specific details as possible, and let each person explain his or her drawing to you.

- If an employee is finding it difficult to identify his or her preferences, it may help to set up situations that contrast the differences. For example, have the person try doing a portion of work in a brightly lit room and another portion in an area where the lights are lower. Ask which lighting made it easier to concentrate. Be prepared for the answer "It doesn't matter." Remember that sometimes it really *doesn't* matter.

Find the drawing you made when you finished the last chapter. Now add some elements that show your environmental preferences. Do you need a lot of light? Do you need the room to be warm? Can you work if you're hungry?

IN A NUTSHELL

Not everyone benefits from the same surroundings when concentrating on work. The bottom line is this: Do you know what works for you? Do you know what works for your organization as a whole? Would you be willing to change your idea of what a standard workplace looks like? If you would, you might discover that more work gets done in an environment that fits an employee's individual learning style. You may even learn that some of us *need* chaos to accomplish order!

Chapter Eight
HOW DO WE REMEMBER?

floccipaucinilihilipilification
(The act of estimating something as worthless)
—Oxford English Dictionary

How long would it take you to learn to spell the word above? How would you remember it? Would it be important for you to hear the word pronounced?

We use a mix of our five senses when processing and memorizing facts and figures. This is called sensory perception. In other words, when we perceive, or take in, information, we're using one or more of our senses to understand and remember it.

This is another dimension that can add to our overall understanding of natural learning style strengths and preferences. While Gregorc's model gave us insight into how our minds work and the Dunns' model showed us the diversity of environmental preferences, this model will help us learn several ways of remembering information.

Take the following test to determine if you're an auditory, visual, or kinesthetic learner.

LEARNING PREFERENCES CHECKLIST

Place a check mark by all the statements that strongly describe what you prefer.

Auditory

__I need to hear myself say it in order to remember it.

__I often need to talk through a problem aloud in order to solve it.

__I memorize best by repeating the information aloud or to myself over and over.

__I remember best when the information fits into a rhythmic or musical pattern.

__I would rather listen to a recording of a book than sit and read it.

Visual

__I need to see an illustration of what I'm being taught before I understand it.

__I am drawn to flashy, colorful, visually stimulating objects.

__I almost always prefer books that include pictures or illustrations with the text.

__I look like I'm daydreaming when I'm trying to get a mental picture of what's being said.

__I usually remember better when I can actually see the person who's talking.

Kinesthetic

__I have difficulty sitting still for more than a few minutes.

__I usually learn best by physically participating in a task.

__I almost always have some part of my body in motion.

__I prefer to read books or hear stories that are full of action.

__I remember best when I can do something with the information.

SENSORY MODALITIES

Those three types of sensory perception, called modalities, have been studied in detail by learning-styles researchers Walter Barbe and Raymond Swassing.[1] We all use all three in varying degrees. Let's take a closer look at each of them.

AUDITORY Learning by listening to verbal instructions; remembering by forming the sounds of words.

If you're a strong auditory learner, that does not necessarily mean you only need to hear something once to remember it. It does mean that in most circumstances, you need to hear yourself say it in order to effectively commit it to memory. If your auditory mode is particularly strong, you may find yourself reading aloud instead of silently and repeating instructions to make sure you understand them. At the grocery store, you may find that people avoid your aisle because even though you're all alone, you're talking out loud. No, you're not crazy; maybe you just need to verbalize your shopping list.

During my years as a police officer, one of my specialties was finding and arresting drunk drivers. A crucial part of determining whether a driver was too intoxicated to be behind the wheel was the field sobriety test. After I put the suspected drunk driver through a variety of balance tests, I always asked the same question at the end: "Could you please say the alphabet for me?"

Unless you're a rare case or a hardened alcoholic, you usually can't say the alphabet at a normal conversational rate if you're under the influence. If drunk driving weren't so serious, it would have been almost amusing to hear the various versions of the standard alphabet those inebriated individuals recited. Interestingly, it seems that no matter how drunk a person is, he or she can almost always sing the alphabet song because of the auditory sing-song rhythm. I had more than one person in a business suit standing by the side of the road and singing his ABCs just so he could remember how the alphabet started!

The strong auditory learners in your office may often think aloud and need to talk things through. Be careful when you listen—make sure they've actually reached their final conclusion before you act on what they say.

VISUAL   Learning by seeing and watching; using strong visual associations.

If the visual way of learning is particularly strong for you, you may need to picture in your mind what you're learning. You may often be accused of daydreaming or being lost in thought. The more visual learner usually learns best by associating pictures with the words or concepts being used. When reading or remembering, the visual learner may constantly be imagining what things look like and may sometimes be picturing something very different from the actual facts.

Because I'm a strong visual learner, I began to keep a written record of the names of places that evoked strong mental pictures, even though I realized the images in my mind were probably not entirely accurate. For example, I get a warm, full feeling when I see the street sign in Nampa, Idaho, that tells me I'm driving down Chicken Dinner Road. It's not a very positive image that pops into my mind, however, when I read the name of one of the long-standing used-car lots in Boise: Fairly Reliable Bob's. But by far my most vivid visual image comes when I drive south of downtown Seattle past a large brown building sporting a big sign identifying it as the Buffalo Sanitary Wipers Company. Wow! Talk about mental images!

Your more visual colleagues may say things like "Show me what you mean" or "I just can't see it happening." If you believe you're dealing with a visual learner, try to reinforce what you talk about with something written. For example, after an important phone call, send the person a fax summary of what you discussed.

KINESTHETIC Learning by becoming physically involved and actually doing something with what's being learned.

If you were a child whose *kinesthetic* modality was strongest, you may have been in almost constant motion. All your life you have probably been accused of being "fidgety" or a "wiggle worm." The kinesthetic person hears things like "Sit still!" "Put your feet on the floor!" "No more trips to the drinking fountain!" Although most teachers and parents work hard to get children to be still, the strong kinesthetic child needs to put some sort of action to the learning or the learning doesn't stick! Even if the action is as simple as pacing or moving while reading or memorizing, the strongly kinesthetic learner will remember best what he or she learned while on the move.

Anne, a very kinesthetic friend of mine (now a physical education teacher!), admitted that her parents were pretty frustrated with her seemingly endless movements. Her mother would insist Anne stay in her bedroom in the basement until all her homework was done. Finally, this resourceful and restless learner devised a way to learn and still keep moving. She used the basement stairs. For spelling or vocabulary, each stair was a letter or word. For history, each was an important fact or date. For geography, each became a different location. Her mother was puzzled as to why Anne was constantly pounding up and down the stairs. All she knew was that Anne's homework was being done and her grades were improving!

Most strongly kinesthetic people are only able to concentrate on one thing for about ten minutes at a time without taking some sort of break. Since physical activity is so important, if you are highly kinesthetic, you may want to put your work on a clipboard and do it "on the run." Be sure you make your deadline for the work to be finished, and burn up energy while working! When you must memorize important information, try associating some sort of bodily movement with what needs to be remembered.

TRYING DIFFERENT MODALITIES

Often without even realizing it, we use our strongest modality when dealing with others. By deliberately trying some strategies for all modalities, you may find your effectiveness greatly increased. Let me give you some ideas to help you identify and use several different approaches for all three modalities as you deal with your colleagues and clients.

You're encouraging someone to learn or process *auditorily* if you

- use discussion and brainstorming sessions.
- repeat what you say without putting it in writing or drawing a picture.

- use music, poetry, or rhythm to get your message across.
- read aloud to someone.
- use others as a sounding board as you talk through ideas or plans.

You're encouraging someone to learn or process *visually* if you

- use even a rough sketch to make sure others can see what you mean.
- use bright, stimulating colors in folders, notebooks, and presentations.
- use outlines and agendas for meetings or presentations.
- use charts and graphs to make your point.
- ask someone to read brochures and other promotional literature.
- spark the imagination by using descriptive language.

You're encouraging someone to learn or process *kinesthetically* if you

- require physical activity to accomplish a goal.
- design activities or projects to be done in short spurts.
- create a relaxed, informal work environment.
- allow for frequent breaks or changes of environment.
- use big spaces for writing or drawing.

Art supplies   Picture

Schedule board

Poster

There are three ways in which we take in and remember information. They are: auditory, visual, and kinesthetic. Add to your picture elements that illustrate how you take in information. You can be a CS, an AS, an AR, or a CR and can take in information in any of the three ways listed above. Now let's see what the AR in our example does. He is a strongly visual AR learner.

┌─ **IN A NUTSHELL** ──────────────────────────────┐

Most people find they're strong in at least two of the modalities, and maybe even all three. No one is restricted to just one modality strength. If you aren't sure whether the auditory, visual, or kinesthetic method would work best for you, try out each approach until you find the one that fits. It may even vary from day to day. The important thing is to find the method of remembering and reviewing that works best for each individual.

└──┘

Chapter Nine
HOW DO WE UNDERSTAND?

"Can you tell me where to find the library?"

"Sure! Just go two blocks to the park with the statue in the middle, you know—where they tore up the road last year. Take a right until you get just past the fire station, then go about three more blocks until you see a great big white house with a green picket fence. The library is right across the street."

"I'm sorry, I'm a little confused. Can you tell me street names? Can you give me the address of the library?"

"Huh? Nope. Sorry—I only know how to get there!"

We have already looked at several ways to identify learning styles. The contents of this chapter can give you a solid grasp of the way you assimilate information from the very beginning. When we learn, a fundamental difference occurs in the way each of us takes in and communicates data, as we can see in the scenario above. The Witkin model of learning styles can help us recognize and appreciate this process.

This chapter will help you understand that learners of all ages can benefit by recognizing and using inborn learning strengths for tackling almost any task, assignment, or test. As we focus on various training situations, you may find unexpected reasons why you or your colleagues are experiencing either success or frustration when it comes to learning.

During World War II, the United States Navy made a startling discovery about its fighter pilots. All those pilots were exceptionally intelligent, incredibly talented, extremely motivated, rigidly screened, and thoroughly trained. However, when flying through a fog bank, some of them would fly out of the mist *upside down*. This *concerned* the navy! It couldn't afford to have pilots in the air who lost their whole sense of being upright when they lost their external field of vision.

The navy called in a psychological researcher, Herman Witkin,[1] to conduct tests on the pilots to determine which ones should be flying and which ones needed additional instrument training before they got into any more clouds.

Witkin designed a special room for his experiments. He placed each pilot in a chair that tilted inside a room that also tilted independent of the chair. When the pilot was sure he was sitting straight up and down, he was to tell Witkin. Some of these pilots would claim they were sitting straight, and yet when Witkin checked, they were actually tilted—sometimes as much as thirty degrees! They needed the room to be lined up with them in order to feel they were *sitting* straight.

It's a lot like the sensation you get at Disneyland's theater in the round. You're clutching the railing, trying to keep from falling off the back of that fire truck you see on the screen. If the lights in the theater came on, you might feel a little silly! Nothing is actually moving. You're standing still, and the only thing that's really changed is your external field of vision, but it can still affect whether you feel you're standing straight up or leaning.

Other pilots tested by Witkin *always* knew when they were sitting straight up, no matter how tilted the room was. Evidently they were not affected as much by their external field of vision as the disoriented pilots.

This experiment began strictly as a test of physical perception. But almost by accident, Witkin and his associates began to notice some behaviors and traits that were consistent between the two types of pilots and the way in which they approached learning tasks. The pilots who always knew when they were sitting straight up tended to be more *field independent,* or *analytic,* when learning new information. They automatically broke down any information given them into component parts and then focused on details.

The other pilots, those who needed their external field of vision in order to know when they were sitting straight, tended to approach information in a much more *field dependent,* or *global,* way. They got the overall picture, or "gist," of things, but they didn't worry about the details as much. Remember, both types of pilots were intelligent, talented, and motivated. The difference lay not in whether they *could* learn but in how they naturally learned *best.*

Because each person sees the world from his or her own frame of reference, it stands to reason that even in situations where many people see the same event, they'll have several versions of what actually happened.

As a police officer, I helped investigate many automobile accidents. I would pull up to the accident scene, locate witnesses, and then begin the challenge of finding out what actually happened. The first witness might give me an accurate description of the cars involved—the years, the makes, the models, the colors. The next witness wouldn't have a clue about the cars involved but would launch into a detailed description of the drivers. The third witness would look a little embarrassed at not noticing the cars and drivers but couldn't wait to relate how the accident *happened.*

Did those people see the same accident? Yes, but their varying perspectives reflect the same learning differences the pilots experienced. The witnesses were looking at the situation through their own "windows." The analytics were automatically recording details in their minds; the globals were more concerned with the overall picture of what had happened.

That same natural tendency toward being either more *global* or more *analytic* also greatly influences the way we approach learning and the effectiveness of our training. Of course, no one person is purely one style or the other. But if we can identify some strengths and natural inclinations, we may discover more efficient ways to study and learn.

The following informal survey will help you determine your natural global or analytic strengths. Answer as honestly as possible, and even though you may want to choose both options on any given statement, always try to choose the one you would do *most* of the time.

What's My Dominant Learning Style?

Place a check mark beside the *one* statement in each pair that best describes your preferences *when you are learning.* When you are learning, do you *usually*

    A B

1. __   like learning by yourself better than working with another person or group?

       __ like learning with another person or group better than working by yourself?

2. __   finish one job before going on to the next one?

       __ begin a new job even if you have not finished an earlier one?

3. __   begin your work without waiting to see how someone else does it?

       __ prefer to wait for someone else to start before you begin?

4. __   find it easier to remember details when you read than to remember main ideas?

       __ find it easier to remember main ideas when you read than to remember details?

5. __   prefer true-false and multiple choice tests with one right answer?

       __ prefer tests that ask you to explain reasons and write out answers?

6. __   need to have your desk and work area neat to concentrate?

       __ find you can get your work done even if your desk or work area is cluttered?

7. __   feel your time was wasted if the teacher doesn't put a grade on work you turned in?

       __ not mind the teacher not giving you a grade as long as your work was recognized?

8. __ prefer competing on your own to competing on a team?

__ prefer competing on a team to competing on your own?

9. __ prefer to have choices as to how to accomplish assignments you're given?

__ prefer that the teacher tells you exactly how the assignment should be done?

10. __ want to go over a test that's been graded in order to correct what you missed?

__ want to look over your graded test but do not want to correct specific answers?

11. __ find it fairly easy to ignore distractions while you work or study?

__ find it pretty difficult to ignore distractions while you work or study?

12. __ prefer to have an assignment in smaller parts and given step-by-step?

__ need to know the whole assignment before you work on parts or steps?

13. __ prefer to think about a decision and figure out what to do by yourself?

__ ask other people's opinions if you aren't sure about making a decision?

14. __ not take it personally if someone tells you you've done something wrong?

__ automatically take it personally if someone says you've done something wrong?

15. __ blame the test if you don't do well and you studied what the teacher told you?

__ blame yourself if you don't do well on a test and you studied what the teacher said?

__ __ **Column Totals**

Total the number of check marks in each column. If the number is greater in column A, you tend to be more *analytic*. If the number is greater in column B, you tend to be more *global*.

Although you got a higher number in one column, remember there is no *pure* style. All of us are a mixture of many style characteristics. The terms global and analytic are extremes, and most of us will find ourselves to some extent in both categories. Remember, too, that how you came out on the Gregorc model will influence the type of *global* or *analytic* learner you are. For example, there's a big difference between an analytic who is Abstract Random and an analytic who's Concrete Sequential!

My husband, John, is extremely analytic by nature. When we watch a movie together, he must watch *every single* credit go by at the end. He reads each name and notes each line of information. If you ask him later what the movie was about, be prepared to hear a *lengthy* retelling of the story, complete with snippets of dialogue.

I watched the same movie. But because I'm a more global learner, if you asked *me* what the movie was about, I would probably give you a general and vague description of the plot. Who starred in the movie? I don't know—some tall guy with brown hair who works on a TV show. Where was the movie filmed? I don't know—big city, tall buildings, snow on the ground. After all, you didn't tell me there was going to be a *quiz* at the end! You see, I just *experienced* the movie. I don't pay attention to specific details unless you tell me ahead of time what I'm supposed to be looking for.

The person who is a more global learner sees the *big picture,* or overall view, while the analytic focuses on the *parts* that make up the big picture. A more analytic learner figures you have to clearly understand the parts to eventually understand the whole. The more global learner claims there's no point in clarifying a detail if you can't see where it fits into the big picture. The global sees all the parts as being related to each other and may have trouble breaking them out separately.

It's a lot like putting together a jigsaw puzzle. As a global, I must constantly see the picture on the box in order to put the individual pieces together. But my analytic husband often prefers to determine how the shapes of the pieces fit together. He may put several sections of the puzzle together before he ever concerns himself with how everything fits into the completed picture.

When training firemen and policemen to write reports, I've found it's often easy to identify their learning-style strengths based on what they include or leave out of their reports. For example, dominant globals tend to leave out important details. They write as though the reader were there. Analytics, on the other hand, usually include plenty of details, but they sometimes lose sight of what the details were supposed to prove. For both styles, it's important to understand what comes naturally when they're dealing with information.

Now that you've filled out the informal checklist, let's take a look at some characteristics that can help you pinpoint whether your dominant style is analytic or global. It *is* possible to be right in the middle. Remember, this has to do *only* with how you interact with *information,* not necessarily how your global or analytic tendencies may show up in interpersonal relationships.

HOW ANALYTIC ARE YOU?

ANALYTIC STRENGTHS

- details
- focus
- organization
- specifics
- direct answers
- consistency
- sense of justice
- objectivity
- individual competition
- doing one thing at a time

WHAT YOU SHOULD KNOW ABOUT THE ANALYTIC STYLE

- likes things ordered in a step-by-step way
- pays close attention to details
- must be prepared
- needs to know what to expect
- often values facts over feelings
- prefers to finish one thing at a time
- resists becoming personally or emotionally involved
- is highly logical
- is self-motivated
- finds the facts but sometimes misses the main idea

ANALYTIC FRUSTRATIONS

- having opinion expressed as fact

- not understanding the purpose for doing something
- not understanding how they will be evaluated
- listening to an overview without knowing the steps involved
- listening to an explanation when all that's needed is a yes or no answer
- dealing with generalities
- having to find personal meaning in all that they learn
- not finishing one task before going on to the next

HOW GLOBAL ARE YOU?

GLOBAL STRENGTHS

- seeing the big picture
- valuing relationships
- cooperating in group efforts
- reading between the lines
- maintaining a sense of fairness
- seeing many options
- paraphrasing
- doing several things at once
- giving and receiving praise
- reading body language
- getting others involved

WHAT YOU SHOULD KNOW ABOUT THE GLOBAL STYLE

- is sensitive to other people's feelings
- is flexible

- goes with the flow
- learns by discussion and working with others
- needs reassurance and reinforcement
- works hard to please others
- takes all criticism personally
- avoids individual competition
- tries to avoid conflict
- may skip steps and details

GLOBAL FRUSTRATIONS

- having to explain themselves analytically
- not getting a chance to explain themselves at all
- not knowing the meaning for doing something
- having to go step-by-step without knowing where they'll end up
- not being able to relate what they are learning to their own lives
- not receiving enough credit for their effort
- having to show the logical steps they used to get an answer
- accepting criticism without taking it personally
- people who are insensitive to other people's feelings

Whether we're more global or more analytic, we tend to assume that others want us to give them information the same way we ourselves would like to receive it. In our home, I'm frequently guilty of ignoring John's need for specific information in favor of my more general outlook. A classic example happened once when he asked me where to find a particular item. "It's in the other room," I told him.

He just looked at me and blinked. "What other room?" he asked.

"The dining room."

"*Where* in the dining room?"

"The rolltop desk."

"*In* the rolltop desk or *on* it?"

"In it, I think."

"Toward the front or toward the back?"

"Toward the back."

"On the left or on the right?"

"On the left."

That incident happened a long time ago, and I've learned more about how an analytic mind expects to receive information. Now when John asks me where something is, I pause for a moment. Then I say something like, "I think it's in the kitchen cupboard to the left of the stove on the middle shelf toward the back on the right."

He looks at me with a grateful smile and says, "*Thank you* for being so specific!"

I may *not* know exactly where the item is, but I know it's close to the place I said. I've discovered that if I start out with very specific information, John doesn't mind continuing the search!

Since the model deals specifically with how we understand information, let's take a look at the differences between global and analytic, especially when you find yourself in training situations where you must become a classroom learner again.

PAYING ATTENTION

Learning style differences show up most during technical training. Those who find themselves faced with the task of mastering a new computer system or learning an entirely different billing format often feel confused and overwhelmingly frustrated. If you've done technical training, you've probably seen some people in your audience shaking their heads in resignation while others looked dazed. When you ask students to demonstrate what they've learned in the session, they can't do it. Haven't they been paying attention? Yes, they have, but they just don't get it, because our naturally dominant learning style affects how we listen, what we pay attention to, and what we remember.

When global learners first hear new information, they take it in by listening for the "gist" of what's being said. They may find themselves mentally ahead of the speaker because they catch on quickly. But because it isn't natural for them to listen for specific details, it may appear that they haven't been paying attention at all. They've listened, and what they're getting is general impressions and an overall idea of what's being said. Unless global learners train themselves to listen for details, they may miss significant pieces of what's being taught.

It's not unusual to hear globals come out of a meeting or workshop saying, "Wow! That was just what I needed to hear." But when you ask, "What was it about?" they'll hesitate and say, "You didn't tell me I was going to have to tell you what it was about!" In any situation where globals are taking in new information, they need to know *going in* what to listen for. It's almost impossible for them to reconstruct the details later.

Analytics take in new information very differently. When they first hear it, they listen for specific details. Later they may even be able to tell you the exact words a speaker said. While they're very good at details, it's sometimes difficult for them to identify the overall *concept* of the information. For example, analytic learners may be able to relate all the specific steps in a certain procedure but not be able to explain what the procedure accomplishes. Analytics must consciously stretch to understand and even to see the bigger picture.

TEACHING FOR UNDERSTANDING

A highly qualified instructor was explaining the merits of a newly released software program. It had been designed to help emergency dispatchers communicate quickly with technicians in the field. As the details of the complex and sophisticated procedure were outlined, I noticed the questions followed a distinct pattern when asked by analytics and another pattern when asked by globals. The analytics focused immediately on the technical instructions. How should data be input? Which codes produced which messages? How soon could this program go on line?

The globals seemed a little distracted by the details. The instructor hadn't given much background about how the program had been created. The globals were asking, "Whose idea was this?" "How has it been working for other organizations?" "How hard will it be to retrain the people who'll use it?"

For training to be as effective as possible, an instructor must consider both analytic and global perspectives. If you find yourself training a diverse group of learners, give both details *and* background (even if the background review is brief) for what you're teaching. Although providing this information may seem like a lot of extra work at first, you'll soon see how it pays off in having both globals and analytics understand the information the first time through.

If you're the one being trained, quickly try to identify which parts are easiest for you and which are most frustrating. See if you can figure out the training instructor's teaching style and determine if it's compatible with your natural learning style. By identifying specific areas where your style and the trainer's are different, you may be able to depersonalize the frustration you feel and increase your ability to stretch your style to accomplish maximum learning.

ORGANIZATION AND TIME MANAGEMENT

Jeanette's desk looked cluttered, as usual. As Rob paused to talk to her, he noticed a new organizer/binder on top of her "to be filed" stack. "Hey, Jeanette, isn't that the expensive organizer you bought last month?" he asked.

Jeanette shrugged and kept on working. "Oh, yeah," she replied. "They told me it would organize me. But yesterday I realized that at some point I would have to organize *it*. So I'm going back to my old way."

What kind of learning style do you suppose a person who teaches time-management classes might have? You're right—analytic! And who do you suppose *takes* those time-management classes? Right again—globals! Although both styles can be successfully organized, they usually have very different views of how organization and time management look. Is it any wonder, then, that the standard methods employed in business usually don't work for everyone?

It makes the most sense to analytics to have a place for everything and everything in its place. Globals, on the other hand, usually consider themselves organized if they're able to *find* something when they need it, even if they have to rummage through a whole pile of stuff to get it. Though globals may not *appear* to be organized, you may be surprised at how quickly they can locate what they need.

Because traditional organization and time-management systems are analytically structured, they fit with the analytic learner's style and are greatly valued. A more global learner may struggle if organizing notebooks and materials is part of the job requirements of an analytic employer.

If you supervise global employees who seem to be constantly disorganized, try to help them understand the *need* to be organized. If the purpose is to be able to locate any papers or materials later, globals need to make sure their system (even if it looks messy and disorganized to you) helps them do that. A good test is whether they can find any paper that's needed in sixty seconds or less. If they can, obviously the system works, no matter how it looks. If they can't, the system needs to be changed.

When it comes to improving in the areas of time management and organization, globals and analytics struggle with different kinds of problems. On the following pages, you'll find some of the most consistent areas of frustration for both styles and some practical ways of dealing with those frustrations.

THE DOMINANT ANALYTIC

It's hard to work with interruptions. Because the natural bent of the dominant analytic mind is to learn by thinking about one thing at a time, it's very disruptive to analytics' concentration to be focused on a concept or an idea and then suddenly to have to think about something else. If you think of something for analytics to do or something you need to say before their current task is finished, don't break their concentration by interrupting. Write it down, and talk with them after they finish.

There are too many places to organize at once. Dominant analytics are almost always more efficient when tasks can be divided into categories or pieces. These people get a much greater sense of accomplishment from making a big difference in a small place rather than barely making a small difference in a big place.

Just before John and I got married several years ago, my global nature was running wild with random thoughts and last-minute tasks. I kept mentioning things to John, my analytic bridegroom, like "Don't forget you promised to mow the lawn before your mother arrives," "Did you call that man about the contract negotiation?" and "Will you pick up the rings while you're in North Seattle?" Finally, John said, "Cindy, just make me a list."

Well, I sat down and wrote out a beautiful to-do list. I printed every item neatly, numbered each one, and put a space in front of the number so he could check it off after he had accomplished the task. I proudly presented my list, and John politely thanked me.

A few minutes later, as I walked through the dining room, I saw John sitting at the table, recopying my list! "What's wrong with my list?" I asked.

He held up the piece of paper he was using to recopy the original list. The paper was neatly divided into four categories: Personal, Wedding, Business, and Miscellaneous. "You have everything clumped together on the same list," he replied a little incredulously. "You shouldn't have put contract negotiation—a necessary business task—and mowing the lawn—a nice thing to get done if there's time—on the same nonspecific list!"

Once he had sorted my list, he began to work in earnest on accomplishing the tasks.

There needs to be some sort of system. Dominant analytics work best when there's a definite and consistent method of doing things, especially if they can create the system themselves. Keeping a daily schedule and/or list of things to do often helps them maintain a sense of structure and predictability. Analytics are usually most comfortable when they can set and meet specific goals, preferably every day.

THE DOMINANT GLOBAL

It's easier to get an organizational system than to keep it. Dominant globals often have what could be called a "pile and bulldoze" system of organizing papers and materials. They start out with all the best intentions of filing things away, but after they find and use something, they frequently toss it into a to-be-filed box, intending to put it where it belongs later. Before they know it, there's a huge pile of papers that practically needs to be bulldozed.

A helpful tip is to simplify the system as much as possible so it will be easy for them to put things back. Big baskets or colorful files that hold very general categories of things will encourage at least getting papers back in the right area.

Once in a while, even globals can become overwhelmed with lack of order. When I finally get to the point of actually cleaning and organizing my office, the first thing I do is take a trip to the store. I have a wonderful time shopping among the colored baskets, plastic drawers, and portable filing systems. When I get back to the office with my bounty, I'm usually out of the mood to organize, and I happily get back to work—in the chaos.

It's too easy to become distracted. The dominantly global mind seems to be going in many directions almost all the time. Just as globals are focused on one task, something else comes up that also has to be taken care of, and instead of finishing the first task, they begin on the new one and work until something *else* distracts them.

One of the best ways to overcome this tendency is for globals to work with another person. They can promise to help each other finish one thing before going on to another. It's surprising how much easier it is to concentrate when someone else is working with you!

"I'll do it" doesn't always mean "I'll do it now." Dominant globals don't always follow through quickly enough for those who have asked them to accomplish a task. Procrastination is a real temptation for globals, and it can cause a lot of conflict with the analytics in their lives. If you want globals to do something *now,* try offering to work with them, at least to get them started. For example, as a global, I often just need a "jump start." If you'll work alongside me even for a few minutes, the chances are good that I'll go ahead and complete the task.

GETTING THE BEST OF THE TEST

As the director of our local reserve police academy for several years, I was usually the first instructor to introduce the cadets to their twelve-week training program. Here were thirty to forty adult men and women who had decided they wanted to be police officers. They had passed the basic-skills test, endured the physical-agility screening, and survived the polygraph. They sat in class the first day feeling that the worst was over. Now we would surely just teach them how to use the lights and sirens and go get the bad guys.

As I passed out the syllabus and agenda, I watched their faces fall. Four weeks of criminal law? Memorize the fourth amendment in its entirety? One hundred fifty spelling words? A test on vocabulary? They thought they'd never have to take tests again once they escaped from school, and here I was telling them they would have to pass a standardized one-hundred-item exam every two weeks if they expected to graduate from the academy. They quickly became very motivated to brush up on their study skills, especially their test-taking techniques.

Although no learning style necessarily *likes* tests, analytics don't seem to feel as threatened or nervous about them as globals do. Globals usually take tests much more personally than their analytic counterparts because they believe the instructor is out to trick them or make them feel dumb. The whole testing situation feels stiff and formal, and sometimes globals do poorly simply because they "psyche" themselves into failing.

Analytics, on the other hand, seem to approach tests with more confidence. Because they automatically break down information into component parts, they have an easier time dividing a test into more manageable pieces. If they dread a test, it's usually because they're not prepared—not because they feel the instructor is out to get them.

One of the biggest frustrations for globals is that they understand the whole concept but struggle with the specific and objective testing techniques that seem to suit analytics perfectly. If globals can gain more confidence in nitty-gritty test-taking skills, they will find they're much smarter than their previous test scores showed.

Both my sister Sandee and I are global. We were talking to a physics teacher when Sandee brought up an interesting question. "If a microwave oven can make things *hot* fast," she asked, "why can't they invent something that would make things *cold* fast?"

The teacher smiled indulgently and stated that it was against the laws of physics. He then patiently defined and explained the applicable law.

When he finished, Sandee echoed the question on my mind: "OK, but if a microwave oven can make things *hot* fast . . ." His definition had just sped over the top of our heads!

My husband, who's a great interpreter in such matters, stepped in. "It's like this," he explained. "Suppose you had a thousand Ping-Pong balls in a net, and the net was tied to the ceiling. If you released the net, the Ping-Pong balls would quickly spread all over the room. That's the concept behind the microwave. To *reverse* the process, you'd have to gather up all the Ping-Pong balls, put them back in the net, and reattach it to the ceiling."

Got it. I still couldn't tell you what the law is *called* or take a test on it to save my life, but I understand the concept of how it *works.* Unfortunately for us globals, we rarely get credit in school for understanding a global concept if we can't pass a test on the analytic details.

I recently asked a group of realtors to give me some test-taking tips that helped them pass their licensing exam. After some discussion, the analytic and global learners who have successfully coped with all sorts of tests shared some of their secrets. It won't be hard to see the difference between their two lists!

TEST TIPS FROM DOMINANT ANALYTIC STUDENTS

- Scan the test quickly to see how many essay, multiple-choice, and true-false questions you'll have to answer. Then divide your time according to how long you have to take the test.
- Do the easy questions first; skip the ones that look hard or complex, and come back to them later.
- Keep your desk or work area completely clear of clutter; it will help you concentrate during the test.
- Always have an extra pen or pencil handy during the test.

TEST TIPS FROM DOMINANT GLOBAL STUDENTS

- Dress comfortably the day of the test.
- Eat something before the test so you won't feel hungry.
- After you've studied for the test, get together with a small group of classmates and review by testing each other.
- Don't come to class too early the day of a test or you may get confused by all the last-minute cramming.

After I gave a presentation at a conference recently, a professional and polished-looking woman came up to speak to me. She was crying as she said, "You're the first person who has really made me feel like I'm not dumb. I'm global!"

Because you are not just a "pure" learning style, add to your picture what you might find in the room that would indicate you are a global or an analytic. Look at our example of a global AR's office to get some ideas.

Stacks of projects
on desk

"Pile & bulldoze"
filing system

Colleague at door
to discuss projects

IN A NUTSHELL

Comprehending information is fundamental to almost everything we do. Knowing if we naturally understand information analytically or globally can help us step outside our dominant style and use a completely different style when necessary. While this is especially important in the academic setting, it's equally important in the areas of business and communication. If I don't comprehend what you say, how can I understand what you mean?

Chapter **Ten**

HOW MANY WAYS CAN WE BE SMART?

Do you feel smart?

How do you even know whether you *are* smart?

Who *decides,* anyway?

For generations, we've been led to believe we should use IQ tests to determine where to place children in school or what kind of programs might be most appropriate. If you've been reading this book in sequence, you've probably already discovered that intelligence comes in *all* learning styles. It doesn't even *look* the same in all styles. Yet we've been trained to value the limited kind of intelligence that conforms to a traditional school system's style of teaching: logic and mathematical skills, verbal and written communication skills, and analytical and organizational abilities. If you happen to be smart in a way that wasn't measured or valued in school, you may have gotten the idea that others are smarter and more successful. *But that just isn't true!*

Many of the things that got you into trouble in school might be the very same things that got you hired later in life. For example, your verbal and social skills earned you a lower citizenship grade because the teacher said you talked too much, but in your job, they make you salesperson of the month. In other words, the traditional school system does little to predict or encourage potential for success outside the classroom.

Several years ago, Howard Gardner, a Harvard professor and eminent researcher, offered compelling evidence that each human being possesses *many* intelligences. Each of those intelligences appears to be housed in a different part of the brain. So far, Dr. Gardner has been able to identify seven, and he's still working on identifying others.

Educators, realizing the importance of this research, are beginning to adopt a multifaceted model for schools that incorporates the multiple intelligences. This new model will mean a profound restructuring of public schools in America. Instead of requiring rote drill and repetition of facts, the multiple-intelligence approach helps children learn by gaining hands-on experience through apprenticeships. Instead of simply memorizing facts about civil wars and conflicts, students gain an understanding of why wars happen in the first place and what can be done to prevent them. Without compromising academic outcomes, the multiple-intelligence model can help students succeed in learning by identifying and using their natural intellectual strengths to cope with almost any task.

Since the ability to learn is becoming increasingly important in the business world as well, an understanding and appreciation of the multiple intelligences is essential. This chapter contains a brief overview of Howard Gardner's important research. For a more thorough grasp, read his book *Frames of Mind* and Thomas Armstrong's book *7 Kinds of Smart* (see bibliography).

Unlike other learning style traits we've discussed, Gardner's research claims that intelligence is not fixed at birth, nor does it remain consistent throughout a lifetime. It grows and develops with the passing of time and with the opportunities afforded the individual. We need to recognize and appreciate as many different areas of intelligence as possible within each person. Standard IQ tests may measure how well a person is likely to perform in the current, traditional school system, but the tests don't even come close to predicting a person's potential for success in life after school.

The principal of a private school recently admitted to me that the administration loves the traditional, sequential, well-behaved students. "But," she confided, "we're very *nice* to those students who struggle with academics, because they're often the ones who end up making lots of money and later come back to endow the school!"

EXPLORING THE SEVEN INTELLIGENCES

According to Gardner's findings, everyone can develop a reasonable use of all seven intelligences, although the chances are good that each person tends to shine in two or three and must struggle to become more adept in the others. As you look through the brief descriptions that follow, you'll probably have no trouble identifying those that come easily for you. Regardless of what you may have been taught, any or *all* of these intelligences indicate that you're smart. And remember, no one has to be good at *everything*.

LINGUISTIC Linguistic intelligence has to do with verbal abilities, and those who possess great amounts of this kind of intelligence tend to be very good at writing, reading, speaking, and debating. Many journalists, teachers, and poets find themselves gifted this way. Because conventional IQ tests place a great deal of value on linguistic abilities, a person who is linguistically inclined usually is considered very smart. The more linguistic person often has and uses an extensive vocabulary and tends to be particularly skilled with word games and semantics.

It's not difficult to spot the highly linguistic people in your organization. The chances are good that they speak well and communicate effectively both verbally and in writing. Their vocabulary is frequently larger than the average person's, and they may even (unintentionally) make others feel inadequate when it comes to expressing ideas. They have the gift of *words,* both in understanding them and in communicating with them. They are at their best when they can use illustrations and anecdotes, and they are often excellent storytellers. They are adept at manipulating and sculpting the structure of language, carving out the letters that uniquely capture the heart of the message.

My husband, John, is highly linguistic. He uses language very literally and chooses his words carefully. Early in our dating relationship, we had an argument. I'm not good at apologizing, but in one of my rarer moments, I swallowed my pride and gulped out the words "I'm sorry."

He calmly turned to me and said, "*Sorry* is a statement of condition; *apologize* is the active verb. Now, are you sorry, or do you apologize?"

Although *no* more words were exchanged *that* evening, I had come to realize the importance he placed on phrasing!

Just because you may not be gifted linguistically doesn't mean you can't develop enough linguistic skills to survive and conquer the challenges of a society that values them.

LOGICAL-MATHEMATICAL

Logical-mathematical intelligence has to do with an individual's abilities in numbers, patterns, and logical reasoning. Although I have to admit the very *thought* of this intelligence makes me break out in a cold sweat, I believe everyone needs to possess at least a basic understanding of the tenets of math and logic. If logical-mathematical intelligence comes easily for you, you should score high on traditional IQ tests. Those naturally gifted in this intelligence are often the greatest scientists, mathematicians, and philosophers. On a more practical basis, you need logical-mathematical intelligence to balance a checkbook or grasp the significance of the national debt.

Those who excel in this area of intelligence almost always shine in the areas of budget and finance. Even if their job doesn't specifically deal with numbers or statistics, they will find ways to incorporate this strength into their daily work. They may use their math ability to split the lunch tab evenly or they may help a coworker balance a checkbook. Their logical reasoning skills are highlighted best during a decision-making process. Although working with people who have logical-mathematical skills can be frustrating for those who don't share these strengths, they can provide a much needed objectivity when solving problems.

My more logical and sequential friends are usually horrified to find I don't balance my checkbook. I *do* call the toll-free number periodically to make sure I'm in the ballpark, and I've never bounced a check, but I have real difficulty with the detailed reconciliation form on my bank statement. On the other hand, my mother-in-law balances her bank statement *immediately* upon receipt. For me it's more practical to simply switch banks every couple of years and get a fresh start!

It's important to recognize that logical-mathematical intelligence doesn't mean you have to be a math whiz. So much of our lives involves the mysteries of the scientific universe that most of us don't even realize how much of this intelligence we already use. Maybe if we can stop thinking about numbers and logic in cold, impersonal terms, we can make them more appealing for everyone.

SPATIAL   Spatial intelligence gives you the ability to think in vivid mental pictures, re-creating or restructuring a given image or situation. Those who are gifted spatially can often look at something and instantly pinpoint areas that could be changed to improve its appearance. Highly spatial professions include architecture, drafting, and mechanical engineering. In almost any given situation, those with spatial intelligence have the natural ability to see what something *could* be as easily as others see what it is.

People who demonstrate strong spatial skills often gain a reputation for seeing what others miss. For example, even when dealing with a group of seemingly unrelated images, the spatial person can detect and trace purposeful patterns and designs. They also excel in the area of developing or interpreting graphs and maps. When communicating with a person who has strong spatial ability, you must be careful to paint an accurate and vivid word picture, or you may find your message has been visualized in an entirely different way.

Preparing visual presentations or decorating and arranging an office or room is best left to those with spatial gifts. They have a natural sense of aesthetic balance and symmetrical design. Although their own environment may not always be neat and orderly, they are constantly looking through the large picture window of their mind to organize and rearrange the world.

My statistics professor in college, a man highly gifted spatially, insists that he's basically an *intuitive* person. "For example," he said, "when I drive to a place I've never been before, I look at a map and memorize it visually. As I head to my destination, I mentally bring up the map and 'intuitively' drive right to it."

For those of us who aren't as gifted spatially, it's easy to recognize that this professor's skill in locating his destination has little to do with intuition. It's his acute spatial ability that allows him to visually re-create an accurate map in his mind's eye.

You might recognize a spatial exercise on a standard IQ test as one of those cubes flattened out, with your task being to state which side will be on the bottom when the cube is reconstructed. Does this look familiar?

These squares will fold into a box that is open at the top. Which letter would mark the BOTTOM of the box?

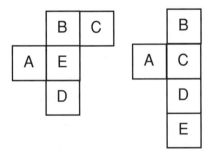

Don't let it make you feel less smart if you can't automatically see the relationships!

MUSICAL　　Musical intelligence expresses itself through a natural rhythm and melody, and one who is gifted in this area often seems to live as if life is set to music. Although you may not have "an ear for music" or perfect pitch, you can still possess a great deal of inherent musical appreciation ability. Many people need music in the background when they're working, and they find themselves tapping their feet almost subconsciously. If you're high in musical intelligence, you may listen to music more analytically than most, appreciating the nuances others may miss altogether.

Cathy, a young mother, told me she felt at a distinct disadvantage with her ten-year-old daughter, Michelle. "Although we're both musically inclined," Cathy said, "Michelle tends to be too analytic for me to really enjoy listening to a performance with her. As we're listening to a classical piece, she'll pause and say, 'There—listen. Do you hear that French horn?' As I'm struggling to pick it out, she's already identifying a 'really cool bass guitar bridge.' And I thought it just sounded like a nice song!"

It's not hard to spot the natural musicians among us. Although many people may be musically gifted, relatively few will make a professional career out of this ability. The colleague who taps out a beat on the desk or the person who hums absentmindedly gives you clues about how important rhythm and music are to his or her well-being. You may find that the musical person is very sensitive to noise, especially less-than-harmonious sounds. Often people with musical intelligence find an outlet for their gift, not in their work, but in hobbies and avocations.

BODILY-KINESTHETIC   Bodily-kinesthetic intelligence reflects a high degree of ability in bodily movement or physical activity. This includes those who can skillfully use their hands, such as surgeons or mechanics; those who so beautifully bring art to life, such as actors, actresses, and artists; and those who vigorously pursue a blend of physical activity and mental strategies, such as athletes and coaches. Although schools are highly enthusiastic about physical education and sports activities, the bodily-kinesthetic intelligence is not often valued as a way of being smart. In fact, sometimes a gifted athlete who can't be as successful linguistically as another student is accused of being a "dumb jock." It's time we recognize and value kinesthetic intelligence instead of considering only quiet academic intelligence an indicator of accomplishment.

The highly bodily-kinesthetic person is usually building or creating something. They have a level of energy and animation that makes other people tired just by watching! It's frustrating for those who are not kinesthetic that this highly active person is almost never at his or her desk. People are constantly trying to track this individual down. They are forced to leave a trail of messages in an attempt to catch up with him or her. The kinesthetic person will not stand still and look you in the eye while you are conversing. These people prefer to stay on the move, listening to you while simultaneously doing at least one or two other tasks. If your organization wants to make steady progress, the bodily-kinesthetic person can certainly help you keep things moving!

Two adult sisters came to me after a seminar I had given on the subject of multiple intelligences. They had tears in their eyes as they related the story of their dad, who had dropped out of school in the eighth grade and gone on to earn a living as a wood-worker. His cabinetry and furniture were absolutely flawless and in great demand. Even though his workmanship showed great kinesthetic intelligence, he had always felt inadequate. His self-esteem had suffered for years because he was convinced it's not possible to be smart if you don't complete school.

Bodily-kinesthetic people can often "feel things in their bones," and their lives are full of physical activity. The more we try to force these folks to sit still, the more restless their minds become, and the less effective formal instruction can be. Instead of fighting their need to move, we should find ways to channel this energy into positive learning.

INTERPERSONAL Interpersonal intelligence affords those who have it the gift of understanding, appreciating, and getting along well with other people. This intelligence isn't usually measured in the traditional academic setting, and those who possess it often find themselves in trouble for using it! These people have a sixth sense when it comes to reading another person. They can almost always tell when something's wrong, even if no words have been spoken. Those who need a friend are quickly drawn to the person with interpersonal intelligence.

Every organization needs at least one, if not several, employees who possess an extraordinary amount of people skills. These interpersonally gifted people can intuitively encourage, motivate, and inspire others and are valuable team members to have when you need to present a positive corporate image and maintain a healthy work environment. Those who exhibit high interpersonal intelligence often find that others are drawn to them as confidants. They are the ones who offer affirmation, praise, and advice to colleagues. Their nurturing abilities often provide the "glue" that holds the team together.

Because they thrive on relationships, it is very difficult for the highly interpersonal person to work alone or to work among people who don't get along with each other. As students they may have gotten into trouble for talking too much, but in the workplace, their interpersonal skills may be one of their very best assets.

Many of those in such helping professions as counseling, social work, and ministry find themselves relying heavily on their interpersonal abilities. Although they can work on developing this intelligence, they may well remain very uncomfortable with the demands of such jobs if they're not naturally gifted interpersonally.

INTRAPERSONAL

Intrapersonal intelligence isn't always readily apparent in a person because it so often expresses itself in solitude. It's a natural gift of understanding ourselves, knowing who and what we are and how we fit into the greater scheme of the universe. Those who are naturally strong intrapersonally enjoy times of reflection, meditation, and seclusion. They seem to possess a more positive self-concept than most, and they don't rely on others' opinions to determine their goals and aspirations.

Although the person who possesses a high degree of intrapersonal intelligence may prefer to spend a great deal of time alone, this independence can also be an invaluable resource to an organization. The objectivity of intrapersonal intelligence allows a person to evaluate, assess, and reflect on information before making decisions. Because this thought process is usually accomplished internally, the intrapersonal individual's silence may be mistaken for ignorance or indifference. Although you may consider someone who is intrapersonal to be uncommunicative, that may not be the case at all. The proverbial "loner" may be sitting on a wealth of information and insight that he or she has not shared, simply because no one has asked for an opinion.

A perfect example of intrapersonal intelligence is found in the book *The Accidental Tourist,* by Anne Tyler. The main character, Macon, said of a woman friend that she talked too much. Macon, on the other hand, was the kind of man who thought silence was better than music. When his wife would switch off the radio, he would say, "Listen, they're playing my song."

Sometimes we misunderstand those who excel in intrapersonal intelligence. We may accuse them of being introverted and shy when those characteristics actually indicate great inner strength.

— IN A NUTSHELL —

No single test can ever measure or predict a person's intelligence. All of us can win when given a chance to show *how* we're smart. The theory of multiple intelligences also helps us value the differences between various cultures. For example, although our culture places a high value on linguistic intelligence, in some areas of the world, that ability would take a backseat to spatial skills. The more we learn to identify and use multiple ways of being smart, the more effective our business and education systems can become in equipping the next generation to deal with the real world.

Chapter Eleven

DOES YOUR JOB PASS
THE STRESS TEST?

My husband was driving me to an early-morning business seminar when I said to him, "I'm working with accountants and bookkeepers today. I've really got to discipline myself to be sequential."

He frowned and said, "I hate it when you do that."

I was surprised. "Why?" I asked.

"Well," he explained, "you come home and dump your stuff inside the door. You don't put anything away or straighten up your messes. You've used up all your sequential discipline on someone else, and you don't have anything left for your own family."

I thought about that. It's true that, like most people, I can be sequential or random, concrete or abstract when I need to be—for a while, at least. But at some point, I run out of strength, and then I'm left with just who I am by nature. If I use every ounce of strength and discipline to be who I'm *not* on the job, when I come home I revert, and my family is stuck with me in my most extreme form—in my case, a global Concrete Random.

Recently, I was commissioned to instruct a group of city government computer trainers. The trainers were all employed in the accounting department and had very analytic and sequential jobs, so I assumed I would need to be very Concrete Sequential in my presentation. I wasn't far into the training, however, when I discovered that more than half of them were *very* abstract and *very* random.

I expressed my surprise and asked if AR was truly their style. They admitted it was. Then I asked if they really liked their jobs. "No!" they all stated vehemently. So why did they stay? The answers were predictable: Their families counted on the money, there was job security, there were no alternatives, and so forth.

After we discussed the situation, several of those job-mismatched employees confessed they went several days a week, after work, to a bar for "Attitude Adjustment Hour." Many admitted to frequent headaches, ulcers, and other illnesses. Most were sorry to say they argued with their families more than they thought they should and they were under seemingly endless stress.

Here was a group of wonderful individuals whose learning styles didn't match the kind of work they were doing. They felt hopeless about finding a better job niche. They had simply decided to stay stressed and miserable.

The field of behavioral medicine overflows with evidence that happiness and well-being on the job have a great deal to do with our physical and mental health. If you have a job that doesn't use your natural strengths and learning style but rather causes you to consistently use another style, you must continually expend your energy to stretch. It's vitally important to be in a job that fits you and to find the balance between work and home. It has to be a balance that allows you to be yourself most of the time so that, when necessary, you can stretch to accommodate other style demands made on you.

HOW DO YOU FIND YOUR NICHE?

One of the most important reasons for getting to know your own learning style is to make sure you can be at your best as much of the time as possible. For example, are you a more literal, down-to-earth communicator? Do you say what you mean and mean what you say? You'll probably want to avoid jobs that call for a lot of "reading between the lines" or picking up on subtle cues. You may find yourself being misunderstood in situations *you* thought were pretty clear, and frustrated because you got into trouble for something you *didn't* say. On the other hand, you'll find yourself in great demand for those tasks that call for a practical, hands-on approach. Your knack for grasping the obvious may keep every-one's feet on solid ground.

If your inclinations run more toward analysis and research, you may find yourself drawn to positions that call for a careful weighing of options or a deliberate, methodical approach to prob-lem solving. If you end up with a job that calls for the opposite—quick decisions and short answers—your talent for detail and investigation may be misunderstood by your colleagues.

I remember hearing one career-and-outplacement expert make a startling statement. He said that if you asked a group of working Americans the question "Are you in the right job?" only 20 percent would say yes. That's 80 percent of the working public who admit they're not in a job that they feel fits them. They may have a good job, and at times they may feel lucky to have any job, but even high-level executives often find themselves living out their working years in a sort of "quiet desperation" in the hope that retirement may bring some relief or compensation for years of unfulfilling labor.

After reading this book, you may be ready to do some homework in order to learn what kind of job might be suitable for you. Although we won't go into detail here, there are books and resources available to help you match your learning style to the right career. Those resources are listed in the bibliography at the end of this book.

WHAT ABOUT ON-THE-JOB STRESS?

Every job comes with its own brand of stress. What makes the stress unique, however, is the way each person perceives the *cause* of stress.

During my years as a police officer, family and friends thought the greatest stress would be from the life-or-death situations I encountered. Because of my Concrete Random nature, however, mortal peril wasn't nearly as exhausting as the overwhelming amount of detailed paperwork and reports I had to do.

If, as an employer, you try to identify and deal with common causes of job stress, you may find there *are* no universal causes and no universal cures. If you begin to use a learning-styles approach as a framework for placing people in the right positions and identifying what causes them stress, you'll discover that the effectiveness of your staff is often related to how well they fit into their job descriptions. As you design programs for dealing with change and transition, you can adapt the approach to the needs of different learning styles.

DEALING WITH STRESS

When it comes to what causes and relieves stress, each dominant learning style has definite patterns and preferences. Let's look at some of them.

What Keeps Them Happy?

DOMINANT CONCRETE SEQUENTIAL (CS)

- organization
- routine
- clear expectations
- schedules
- tangible rewards
- predictability

DOMINANT ABSTRACT SEQUENTIAL (AS)

- order and purpose
- credible sources of information
- logical outcomes
- opportunities for analysis
- plenty of time to work
- appreciation for their input

DOMINANT ABSTRACT RANDOM (AR)

- frequent praise
- reassurance of personal value and worth
- situations where it's important to work as a team
- opportunities to use creativity and imagination
- acceptance of personal feelings and emotions

DOMINANT CONCRETE RANDOM (CR)

- appreciation for their uniqueness
- independence
- freedom to choose options
- guidelines instead of rules
- opportunities for creative alternatives

What Causes Them Stress?

DOMINANT CONCRETE SEQUENTIAL (CS)

- too much to do
- not knowing where to begin
- no clean, quiet places
- not knowing expectations
- vague or general directions
- not seeing an example

DOMINANT ABSTRACT SEQUENTIAL (AS)

- unreasonable deadlines
- being rushed through anything
- not having hard questions answered
- abiding by sentimental decisions
- being asked to specifically state emotions

DOMINANT ABSTRACT RANDOM (AR)

- having to justify feelings
- competing individually
- not feeling liked or appreciated
- pressure to be more sequential
- lack of harmony among everyone in the workplace

DOMINANT CONCRETE RANDOM (CR)

- excessive restrictions and limitations
- forced schedules or routines
- not being appreciated as unique individuals
- not being given credit for knowing the right thing to do

How Can You Help?

DOMINANT CONCRETE SEQUENTIAL (CS)

- give specific time and space for quiet, uninterrupted work
- ask what you can do to help
- provide a concrete example of what's expected
- be as specific and literal as possible in all your communication

DOMINANT ABSTRACT SEQUENTIAL (AS)

- provide additional time to complete tasks
- give lots of uncluttered space and quiet time to work
- put as much as possible in writing
- appreciate the less emotional aspects of a situation

DOMINANT ABSTRACT RANDOM (AR)

- allow them to work together with someone as a team
- notice the good things without pointing out the bad
- give daily reassurance of their value to the organization and the world
- listen without offering unsolicited advice

DOMINANT CONCRETE RANDOM (CR)

- lighten up! (A sense of humor can go a long way)
- back off, and don't force the issue
- help them figure out what will inspire them
- encourage finding lots of ways to reach the same goal

What Should You Avoid Doing?

DOMINANT CONCRETE SEQUENTIAL (CS)

- telling them to "just relax and forget about it for a while"
- reminding them that "life's too short"
- quipping that they "shouldn't sweat the small stuff"

DOMINANT ABSTRACT SEQUENTIAL (AS)

- brushing aside their concerns as "no big deal"
- telling them not to worry about it
- reminding them they "think too much"

DOMINANT ABSTRACT RANDOM (AR)

- trying to talk them out of how they feel
- making them feel guilty for expressing emotions
- pointing out how the good "outweighs" the bad

DOMINANT CONCRETE RANDOM (CR)

- trying to make them admit they are experiencing stress
- insisting they "slow down"
- telling them they "do too much already"

PUTTING YOUR STYLE TO WORK

In some ways, it would be nice if we could always work with people who were very much like us in style and perception. In reality, of course, that rarely happens. We can greatly reduce the tension that results from working with opposites, however, just by identifying and understanding what each dominant style values and wants in the day-to-day workplace.

Take a look at the following charts, and you may discover that some of those you work with aren't deliberately trying to annoy and frustrate you!

WHAT DOES THE DOMINANT CONCRETE SEQUENTIAL SUPERVISOR VALUE?	WHAT DOES THE DOMINANT ABSTRACT RANDOM EMPLOYEE WANT?
• results • organization • precision • routines • action • efficiency	• credit for effort • frequent positive feedback • emphasis on high morale • attention to personal aspects • freedom to be spontaneous • opportunities to help others

Do You Foresee Any Conflict Here?

WHAT DOES THE DOMINANT ABSTRACT SEQUENTIAL SUPERVISOR VALUE?	**WHAT DOES THE DOMINANT CONCRETE RANDOM EMPLOYEE WANT?**
• logic • objectivity • theory • statistics • documentation • analysis	• no "unreasonable" restrictions • lots of new ideas • practical reasons for policy • diverse job responsibilities • flexible time schedules • to make a difference

Do You Foresee Any Conflict Here?

WHAT DOES THE DOMINANT ABSTRACT RANDOM SUPERVISOR VALUE?	**WHAT DOES THE DOMINANT CONCRETE SEQUENTIAL EMPLOYEE WANT?**
• harmony • effort • feedback • flexibility • cooperation • loyalty	• specific instructions • schedules and timelines • literal communication • consistent policies • established routines • tangible rewards

Do You Foresee Any Conflict Here?

WHAT DOES THE DOMINANT CONCRETE RANDOM SUPERVISOR VALUE?	WHAT DOES THE DOMINANT ABSTRACT SEQUENTIAL EMPLOYEE WANT?
• ideas	• logical reasons
• enthusiasm	• systematic methods
• intuition	• objective treatment for all
• creativity	• documentation of facts
• innovation	• thorough analysis
• flexibility	• plenty of time

Do You Foresee Any Conflict Here?

Take a moment and look back over the previous charts that demonstrate the differences between supervisors and employees of opposite styles. Did you notice that every characteristic on every chart is positive? They only become negative when they come into conflict with the priorities of the opposite style.

IN A NUTSHELL

I once watched a very tall comedienne bring a very short woman up from the audience to stand beside her. As the two women stood shoulder to waist, the comedienne said to the audience, "You know those pantyhose that say 'One Size Fits All'? Don't you *believe* it!"

There will never be just one approach or program that will fit and be effective for everyone in your organization. What causes one person job stress is often what keeps another person happy. Even if you hate the job you're doing, the chances are good that it's just the right fit for someone else. Invest some time and energy into finding out why you do your job the way you do. Ask yourself these questions:

Am I in the right niche?

Do I know what my most suitable job would be?

Would I recognize it if I saw it?

After reading this book, perhaps you'll discover that the very people on the job who annoy you most are simply working from a learning-styles perspective that's opposite yours. If you can't immediately change jobs, you may be amazed at how much improvement there can be in your current job when you understand what you do best.

Chapter Twelve
A FRAMEWORK FOR SUCCESS

I had just finished giving two days of intensive learning- and communicating-styles training for a large police department. The chief called me into his office to express his appreciation and to make a request. He handed me a list of all his employees, including officers, clerks, and other staff. "I'd like to put all the employees' learning-styles categories in the space beside their names," he said matter-of-factly.

I tried to hide the dismay I felt at his cut-and-dried categorization. But I knew how his learning-styles assessments had come out. "OK," I agreed. "Let's start with your name. What style category should I put beside it?"

He thought for a moment. "I came out AR," he replied. "But actually, my CS was only a couple of points behind. And, truthfully, I'm more analytic than global. And I'm definitely more visual."

He frowned uncomfortably, then sighed. "OK, OK. I get your point," he said. "No *one* category can really describe anyone. But it would be so easy if I could just keep a file in my desk that lets me instantly figure out what style I'm dealing with!"

When we first discover this whole area of learning styles, there's a tendency to label everyone and everything according to one particular style, to categorize and put him or her in a box. But the more you understand about learning styles, the less you'll try to categorize yourself and others. Each person is as unique as his or her fingerprints. Although many fingerprints look basically the same, they're not exactly alike. Sometimes the differences are hard to notice; at other times they're quite obvious.

In this book, I have introduced you to five different learning-styles models to help you understand that each person is a complex and unique combination of natural strengths and preferences. Let's quickly list them for review:

1. Mind Styles (Gregorc)
   Recognizing how the mind works.

2. Environmental Preferences (Dunn and Dunn)
   Designing the ideal work environment.

3. Modalities (Barbe-Swassing)
   Learning strategies for remembering information.

4. Analytic/Global Information Processing (Witkin)
   Identifying effective methods for training and instruction.

5. Multiple Intelligences (Gardner)
   Identifying seven different ways of being smart.

Each of those learning styles adds another dimension to our insights about ourselves and others in our families and ·the workplace. In addition, there are literally hundreds of other learning-styles models. The five I included in this book are my favorites because I've seen firsthand how accurate and practical the results of using them can be and because each has an extremely reliable research base. But now that you've become aware of these learning styles, you'll no doubt find other means of identifying styles in the future. Consider each model or test to be another layer of understanding and not a replacement for the labels you already know.

For many of us, no matter how many learning-styles assessments we take, we find our natural strengths and preferences to be very consistent with one another. For example, my random nature lives with my global style quite compatibly. I don't struggle to understand who I am or what I need in most situations. The obvious drawback to this consistency is that when I need to use characteristics that are *opposites* to my natural strengths, it takes a good deal of discipline and hard work, and it often leaves me feeling frustrated and exhausted.

One of my best friends finds herself strongly random, but she's also very analytical. This causes her a great deal of inner conflict. She needs structure and specific facts for analytic learning, but as a random communicator, she fights regimentation and detail. Once she began to understand learning styles, she could use her seemingly contradictory traits to bring balance to her life. She practiced using her analytical side when she needed to be specific, and she switched to her random side when she needed to see the big picture.

Some people are frustrated that they never seem to fall into *any* definite category on any learning or communicating styles assessments. I usually suggest, lightheartedly, that they're either very well-balanced or really mixed up! They're willing to admit they *feel* mixed up, but with a little more knowledge about and practice of learning styles, they usually begin to see the advantage of switching easily from style to style as circumstances dictate.

One of the most important things to remember about learning styles is that they're *value neutral.* There's no one best style. No single style is any smarter than another, nor is there any style combination that's automatically good or naturally bad. The key lies in how you *use* your natural style strengths and in how willing you are to learn to communicate in a way that may be difficult for you.

The following chart uses the Gregorc model to demonstrate how each of us has a combination of all the different learning-styles characteristics. It will probably be very apparent to you which styles you're drawn to and which you avoid whenever possible!

What a Combination!

WHEN USING YOUR CS STYLE, YOU ARE

- organizing
- sequencing
- paying attention to detail
- following through to the very end
- communicating clearly and concisely

WHEN USING YOUR AS STYLE, YOU ARE

- evaluating information
- analyzing a situation
- figuring out what needs to be done
- researching options
- taking time to be thorough

WHEN USING YOUR AR STYLE, YOU ARE

- sensing what others need
- making life better for everyone
- adapting to almost anything
- bringing harmony amid conflict
- providing love and/or support

WHEN USING YOUR CR STYLE, YOU ARE

- creating new means to an end
- envisioning endless possibilities
- daring to try the unknown
- inspiring others to take action
- believing nothing is impossible

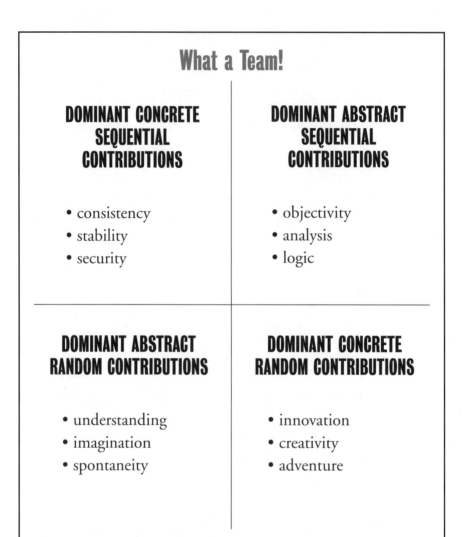

What a Team!

DOMINANT CONCRETE SEQUENTIAL CONTRIBUTIONS

- consistency
- stability
- security

DOMINANT ABSTRACT SEQUENTIAL CONTRIBUTIONS

- objectivity
- analysis
- logic

DOMINANT ABSTRACT RANDOM CONTRIBUTIONS

- understanding
- imagination
- spontaneity

DOMINANT CONCRETE RANDOM CONTRIBUTIONS

- innovation
- creativity
- adventure

LEARNING STYLES AS A FRAMEWORK FOR SUCCESS

The human resources manager looked pleased when I passed her in the hall. She stopped me and said with a smile, "We just had a *great* staff meeting! We were trying this problem-solving process, and Hank was up to his usual thing of pointing out all the various and seemingly endless details involved. Susan stopped Hank and said, 'Boy are you ever being CS today!' Everyone laughed." The HR manager leaned a little closer to emphasize the significance of her last sentence. "Don't you see?" she asked. "We go through this whole scenario every week, and believe me, last week, before the training you gave us, when Hank started talking, we *weren't* laughing."

This particular staff and management team has discovered the value of using a learning-styles approach as a framework for virtually everything it does together. One of the obvious and earliest advantages of using the learning-styles approach when people are working together is the ability to depersonalize conflict between opposite styles. If you say to me, a highly random person, "Cindy, do you think you could be a little more sequential here?" I don't have a problem understanding and accommodating you. We can both smile, knowing that my lack of natural sequential abilities is not a reflection on my intelligence or skills. On the other hand, if you say to me, "Cindy, do you think you could maybe *focus* here for a minute?" I'll probably become defensive and will likely take your question very personally.

Although you'll probably notice an improvement in the way you and your colleagues interact after reading and applying the concepts in this book, it may take some time for you to begin appreciating the value of teamwork between opposite learning styles. As I stated in the first chapter, this is *not* a one-shot method of learning and applying effective communication techniques. Learning styles are so fundamental that they need to become the framework for virtually everything you do.

As business fads and management styles come and go, your knowledge of learning styles can help you evaluate the effectiveness of various methods for different learning styles. Does a program offer enough for all styles? Is the approach biased heavily toward a particular learning style? Can the program be modified to appeal to other styles, or should you choose an approach that's more flexible?

I'd like to show you, briefly, how learning styles can create an effective framework for some of the most important issues we currently deal with in the workplace.

QUALITY IMPROVEMENT: HOW DO YOU DEFINE QUALITY?

A large hospital had taken great care to design and distribute patient surveys over the previous six months. The administration's goal was to determine the quality of care given and use the feedback from patients to improve the level of service throughout the hospital. Unfortunately, the patient surveys did not yield consistent evaluation of services rendered. The administrators had left out one crucial consideration: Patient surveys tend to reflect the patient's learning-styles perspective. For example, the CS may give a grade of A because the service was efficient, the facility was clean and well run, and meals and medications were delivered on time. The AR, on the other hand, may receive the same level of service and yet give a grade of C because there was a lack of personal warmth and attention.

Quality may truly be in the eye of the beholder. Delivering consistent quality can be an almost impossible task if we don't take into account the style of our consumers. When we evaluate our products or services, we must do so from as many different style perspectives as possible.

HUMAN RESOURCES: DISCERNMENT OR DISCRIMINATION?

Sam was a dominant AR who ended up in the world of high finance. He had grown up believing the way to climb the corporate ladder was to enter the realm of management. As an AR, he was already uncomfortable with the incredible amount of facts and details that were part of his job in banking. Because he worked hard and disciplined himself to succeed, however, he was able to convince the senior managers that he was the best person for the job of vice president.

It didn't take long after his promotion for Sam to realize he had definitely made the wrong choice. He needed every ounce of his strength and will to perform his duties. He hated hiring and firing, giving bad news to his employees, and being responsible for multimillion-dollar budgets. His health began to suffer, and his family couldn't understand how this gentle, loving person had turned into such a grouch at home. In less than a year, Sam checked into an alcohol rehabilitation program, and his job was passed on to someone else.

The corporation had spent thousands of dollars to train and groom Sam for the position of vice president. Now his bosses had to begin again with someone new, and they also had to repair the damage done to his employees by Sam's mismatched management style. How could this have been prevented?

The most productive and happiest employees are usually those who are doing what they do best. If we can find nondiscriminatory methods of determining the best fit for individual employees within our organizations, we will likely have people who are consistently working at their best.

When you are hiring someone for a job, your understanding of different style strengths and preferences helps to assure that employees are placed in the best niches for them within your organization. By learning to ask the right questions and listening for answers that will give you insight into the natural design of a person's mind, you can also provide an atmosphere of trust and understanding between you and the people you interview.

CULTURAL DIVERSITY: HOW MUCH IS A MATTER OF STYLE?

"Oh no!" Stan muttered as he opened the memo in his office mailbox. "It's another 'cultural sensitivity' workshop. I *hate* sitting through those things!"

If you've ever heard comments like that, you may be able to turn your colleagues' attitudes around by using the learning-styles framework in your approach to the issues. The concept of learning styles can transcend race, color, creed, religion, and gender, allowing a person to be understood *first* as an individual. Remember, learning styles are only a piece of the puzzle. But if you make the core understanding of another person the identification and appreciation of unique and inborn strengths and abilities, you'll usually find the other pieces of the picture falling into place within a much more positive atmosphere.

You may often find that learning-style differences explain more conflicts between employees than many cultural aspects do.

Remember, the ultimate compliment is to feel understood as an individual. When those in management master the art of treating their employees as individuals with unique and valued strengths, conflict is minimized.

SALES AND MARKETING: HOW DO YOU APPEAL TO DIFFERENT CUSTOMERS?

In a recent training meeting with an automobile manufacturer's service consultants and managers, we were discussing what it would take to establish exclusive customer loyalty to the dealership when it came to servicing their cars. By working through the learning-styles framework we had already established, the group quickly came up with some sound ideas. For example, the CS customer would need financial incentives—coupons, frequent buyer cards, and so on—in order to choose one dealer over another. The AS, however, would need to be convinced of the importance of using original manufacturer's parts, since cost would definitely be a factor. The facts would need to be laid out in writing, and the brochure would need to be well-researched. The AR consumer would need to bond personally with those at the dealership. Then, when he or she did, it would be like cheating on a spouse or trusted friend to go anywhere else. The greatest chance of keeping a CR customer usually lies in the convenience of the service. If the CR never had to keep track of another receipt and yet could have someone keep a detailed and accurate service record for his or her car, the dealership would probably have a customer for life.

Understanding what motivates people to make financial decisions can dramatically increase sales and bottom-line profits. You can design practical and effective strategies for turning people of virtually every learning style into customers. The first chapter of this book told the story of the account executive who didn't consider the differences in style when making his sales presentation. If he had used knowledge of learning styles as the framework for convincing his potential clients of the value of his product, he could have made many more sales and created happy and satisfied customers.

CAN YOU PLEASE EVERYONE?

By now you may be convinced that understanding learning styles will greatly enhance the effectiveness of your organization. But how can you recognize clients' learning styles if you've barely met them and may never see them again? How can you build something into your marketing approach for every learning style? Because it's possible to train your staff to quickly recognize style characteristics, you can do one thing that will immediately ensure you are broadening your appeal in almost every area of sales and marketing. By using the following learning-styles paradigm, you can significantly increase the impact of advertising and public relations as you make sure you're addressing some of the most important issues for each of the four Gregorc learning styles.

A Learning-Styles Paradigm

FOR DOMINANT CONCRETE SEQUENTIALS:

What Will We Accomplish?
Demonstrate tangible results
Define measurable goals

FOR DOMINANT ABSTRACT SEQUENTIALS:

What Will We Learn?
Describe theory and content
Provide evidence of knowledge and credibility

FOR DOMINANT ABSTRACT RANDOMS:

What Difference Will We Make?
Illustrate and emphasize social aspects
Establish positive place in the community

FOR DOMINANT CONCRETE RANDOMS:

What Makes Us Unique?
Provide compelling reasons
Achieve a competitive edge

IN A NUTSHELL

By using basic learning-styles concepts as a framework, you can greatly increase your effectiveness both personally and as an organization. If you truly dedicate yourself to mastering those concepts and using the learning-styles paradigm, you'll see an incredible improvement in virtually every aspect of your business. Although training programs and management techniques may come and go, the individual learning-style strengths and preferences each of us received at birth remain basically consistent. It just makes sense that we address those fundamental differences when we deal with the various facets of business and communication. I believe your knowledge of learning styles can make a profound difference in your organization as you identify and approach *The Way We Work!*

NOTES

CHAPTER TWO

1. Order the *Adult Style Delineator* and *An Adult's Guide to Style* from Anthony F. Gregorc, P. O. Box 351, Columbia, Conn. 06237, or call (203) 228-0093.

CHAPTER SEVEN

1. Kenneth and Rita Dunn are the authors of several books and editors for *Learning Styles Network.* Contact: The Center for the Study of Learning Styles, St. John's University, Jamaica, New York 11439.

CHAPTER EIGHT

1. *The Swassing-Barbe Modality Index.* Administered individually, twenty minutes, all ages. In this test, patterns are presented in each modality and must be retained and repeated. Available from Zaner-Bloser Inc., P. O. Box 16764, Columbus, Ohio 43216.

CHAPTER NINE

1. Herman A. Witkin, "Cognitive Styles in the Educational Setting," *New York University Education Quarterly* (1977), 14–20. Herman A. Witkin, et al., "Field-Dependent and Field-Independent Cognitive Styles and Their Educational Implications," *Review of Educational Research,* 47, 1 (Winter 1977), 1–64.

BIBLIOGRAPHY

Armstrong, Thomas. *7 Kinds of Smart.* New York: Penguin Books, 1993. Using Howard Gardner's model of multiple intelligences, Armstrong provides easily understood descriptions of the seven intelligences, as well as a list of twenty-five ways even an adult can develop each one.

Dunn, Rita, ed. Learning Styles Network. The Center for Learning & Teaching Styles, St. John's University, Jamaica, N.Y. The Learning Styles Network publishes a newsletter, an extensive annotated bibliography, and various materials on learning styles—especially suitable for trainers and educators. (718) 990-6335.

Gardner, Howard. *Frames of Mind: The Theory of Multiple Intelligences.* New York: Basic Books, 1993. A definitive and academic description of Gardner's research of the multiple intelligences theory.

Gregorc, Anthony F. *An Adult's Guide to Style.* Columbia, Conn.: Gregorc Associates, 1982. The definitive volume for identifying and understanding Gregorc's model of learning styles. Packed with definitions and examples, this book is an invaluable reference for serious study.

Isachsen, Olaf, and Linda V. Berens. *Working Together: A Personality-Centered Approach to Management.* Coronado, Calif.:

Neworld Management Press, 1988. A very detailed look at identifying and managing the different personality types in the business world. A valuable reference tool for the serious student of personality and temperament.

Keirsey, David, and Marilyn Bates. *Please Understand Me: Character and Temperament Types.* Del Mar, Calif.: Prometheus, Nemesis, 1978. This book provides a fascinating look at personality type and temperament. You'll discover how your temperament affects your success in relationships, careers, and life in general.

Kroeger, Otto, and Janet M. Thuesen. *Type Talk.* New York: Delacorte Press, 1988. This is a fun, easy-to-read guide to the Myers-Briggs version of Carl Jung's personality types. Loaded with anecdotes, this book is one you'll find yourself loaning to your friends!

————. *Type Talk at Work.* New York: Delacorte Press, 1988. Using the Myers-Briggs personality types, this book is packed with practical applications to the workplace. You'll find guidelines for management as well as specific tips for problem-solving strategies, all designed to make you more effective at work.

Tobias, Cynthia Ulrich, with Nick Walker. *"Who's Gonna Make Me?" Effective Strategies for Dealing with the Strong-Willed Child.* Forty-five minute video. Seattle: Chuck Snyder & Associates, 1992. Focusing on Gregorc's Concrete Random learning style, this video presents practical, hands-on strategies for bringing out the *best* in your strong-willed child. Although aimed at parenting, you'll find this film to be especially helpful in dealing with those "difficult employees."

One of my favorite posters reads:

We have not succeeded in solving all of your problems. The answers we have found only serve to raise a whole new set of questions. In some ways, we feel we are as confused as ever, but we believe we are confused on a higher level and about more important things.

—Author unknown

For more information and to obtain Cynthia Tobias as a speaker or corporate trainer, contact

Learning Styles Unlimited, Inc.
P. O. Box 1450
Sumner, WA 98390

Telephone: (253) 862-6200
Fax: (253) 891-8611

The Significance Principle

The Secret Behind High Performance
People and Organizations

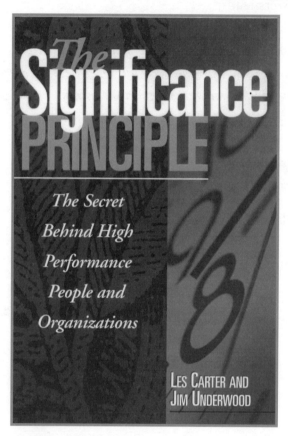

The Secret
Behind High
Performance
People and
Organizations

LES CARTER AND
JIM UNDERWOOD

0-8054-1664-1

The *Significance Principle* is built around the concept of servant leadership. Treating people as though they were important, capable, and valuable encourages them to *perform* that way, achieving higher standards than even they thought possible. This book takes you beyond the pages of the management theory, delivering practical steps of success.

available at your local bookstore